introduction.

If you've been dreaming about a recipe book that delivers sugar-free, low-carb desserts that taste great AND allow you to stick to your grain-free Paleo diet, your dreams just came true! *Keto Sweets* is the second dessert cookbook by Nutritional Therapist Kelsey Ale.

She got the idea to create this book when she saw the growing number of people who were turning to the keto diet to transform their health. She also wanted to be able to offer a book to the dozens of people reaching out to her asking for more diabetic-friendly dessert recipes.

And so *Keto Sweets* was born—it's the perfect cookbook for you or your loved ones who want to balance their blood sugar and shed excess fat while still having their cake and eating it, too!

Within the pages of *Keto Sweets* you'll find a dessert recipe to satisfy any craving—from Peppermint Brownies to Vanilla Cake with Chocolate Buttercream Frosting to White Chocolate Macadamia Nut Cookies to Chocolate Ice Cream—*Keto Sweets* has it all. Every recipe you'll find here is completely grain-free and low-carb, and most can be made completely dairy-free, too! So you can stay on track with fat loss without giving up your grain-free Paleo diet.

Kelsey hopes that you and the people you love will enjoy *Keto Sweets* as much as she enjoyed creating it for you.

Kelsey Ale is a certified Nutritional Therapy Practitioner and Paleo chef/baker living in Santa Monica, California. She discovered her passion for healthy cooking and desserts over 15 years ago. Shortly after, she started running the juice bar at her local health food store, where her love for holistic health began to grow. But she still faced severe health challenges of her own. After discovering how the Paleo diet and other natural lifestyle adjustments helped her heal her own body and recover from illness, Kelsey became fully committed to showing the world how to use delicious food to lose weight, increase mental clarity and energy, and achieve vibrant health.

"Follow me on Instagram and Facebook @thekelseyale to get natural health tips, down-to-earth nutrition advice that works, yummy recipes, and more!"

— Kelsey, www.KelseyAle.com

contents.

Ice Cream

Cake

Frosting

Brownies

Candy

Cookies

Cheesecake

Popsicles

Pies

Panna Cotta & Crème Brûlée

ice cream

Vanilla Ice Cream
Chocolate Ice Cream
Lemon Ice Cream
Strawberry Ice Cream
Mint Chocolate Chip Ice Cream
Salted Chocolate Ice Cream with Almonds
Chai Ice Cream
Avocado Ice Cream

VANILLA ICE CREAM

Prep: 30 mins

Cook/Chill: 6 hrs 30 mins

Total: 7 hrs

Yield: 8 servings

Nutritional info per serving:

Carbs	Fat	Protein
3g	27g	4g

INGREDIENTS:

2 cans full-fat coconut milk (can size 13.5 - 15 oz)

6 egg yolks

¼ cup MCT oil

3 Tbsp granulated erythritol

2 tsp monk fruit powder

2 tsp vanilla

METHOD:

In a medium saucepan, heat the coconut milk over medium heat.

While the coconut milk is warming, combine the egg yolks, MCT oil, erythritol, and monk fruit in a medium mixing bowl, and whisk to completely combine.

When the coconut milk is steaming but not boiling, remove it from the heat and add it to the egg yolks in a slow, thin, steady stream, whisking constantly. Do not add the milk too quickly or it will scramble the egg yolks.

When the coconut milk and egg yolks are completely combined, return the mixture to the saucepan. Add the vanilla and heat over medium-low. Stir constantly until the mixture thickens, about 20 minutes.

When the mixture is somewhat thick, remove it from the heat, and transfer to a clean bowl to cool completely.

Prepare the ice cream according to the ice cream maker instructions. Enjoy immediately like soft-serve, or chill until set.

CHOCOLATE ICE CREAM

Prep: 30 mins

Cook/Chill: 6 hrs 30 mins

Total: 7 hrs

Yield: 8 servings

Nutritional info per serving:

Carbs	Fat	Protein
6g	32g	3g

INGREDIENTS:

2 cans full-fat coconut milk (can size 13.5 - 15 oz)

6 egg yolks

¼ cup MCT oil

3 Tbsp granulated erythritol

6 Tbsp cacao powder

2 tsp monk fruit powder

2 tsp vanilla

METHOD:

In a medium saucepan, heat the coconut milk over medium heat.

While the coconut milk is warming, combine the egg yolks, MCT oil, erythritol, cacao powder, and monk fruit in a medium mixing bowl, and whisk to completely combine.

When the coconut milk is steaming but not boiling, remove it from the heat and add it to the egg yolks in a slow, thin, steady stream, whisking constantly. Do not add the milk too quickly or it will scramble the egg yolks.

When the coconut milk and egg yolks are completely combined, return the mixture to the saucepan. Add the vanilla, and heat over medium-low. Stir constantly until the mixture thickens, about 20 minutes.

When the mixture is somewhat thick, remove it from the heat and transfer to a clean bowl to cool completely.

Prepare the ice cream according to the ice cream maker instructions. Enjoy immediately like soft-serve, or chill until set.

LEMON ICE CREAM

Prep: 30 mins

Cook/Chill: 6 hrs 30 mins

Total: 7 hrs

Yield: 8 servings

Nutritional info per serving:

Carbs	*Fat*	*Protein*
3g	*24g*	*3g*

INGREDIENTS:

2 cans full-fat coconut milk (can size 13.5 - 15 oz), minus ¼ cup

6 egg yolks

¼ cup MCT oil

3 Tbsp granulated erythritol

¼ cup lemon juice

2 tsp monk fruit powder

2 tsp vanilla

1 tsp lemon zest

METHOD:

In a medium saucepan, heat the coconut milk over medium heat.

While the coconut milk is warming, combine the egg yolks, MCT oil, erythritol, lemon juice, and monk fruit in a medium mixing bowl, and whisk to completely combine.

When the coconut milk is steaming but not boiling, remove it from the heat and add it to the egg yolks in a slow, thin, steady stream, whisking constantly. Do not add the milk too quickly or it will scramble the egg yolks.

When the coconut milk and egg yolks are completely combined, return the mixture to the saucepan. Add the vanilla and lemon zest, and heat over medium-low. Stir constantly until the mixture thickens, about 20 minutes.

When the mixture is somewhat thick, remove it from the heat and transfer to a clean bowl to cool completely.

Prepare the ice cream according to the ice cream maker instructions. Enjoy immediately like soft-serve, or chill until set.

STRAWBERRY ICE CREAM

Prep: 30 mins

Cook/Chill: 6 hrs 30 mins

Total: 7 hrs

Yield: 8 servings

Nutritional info per serving:

Carbs	Fat	Protein
3g	27g	4g

INGREDIENTS:

2 cans full-fat coconut milk (can size 13.5 - 15 oz)

6 egg yolks

¼ cup MCT oil

1 Tbsp lemon juice

3 Tbsp granulated erythritol

2 tsp monk fruit powder

1 tsp vanilla

1 cup chopped fresh strawberries

METHOD:

In a medium saucepan, heat the coconut milk over medium heat.

While the coconut milk is warming, combine the egg yolks, MCT oil, lemon juice, erythritol, and monk fruit in a medium mixing bowl, and whisk to completely combine.

When the coconut milk is steaming but not boiling, remove it from the heat and add it to the egg yolks in a slow, thin, steady stream, whisking constantly. Do not add the milk too quickly or it will scramble the egg yolks.

When the coconut milk and egg yolks are completely combined, return the mixture to the saucepan. Add the vanilla and heat over medium-low. Stir constantly until the mixture thickens, about 20 minutes.

When the mixture is somewhat thick, remove it from the heat, and transfer to a clean bowl to cool completely.

Transfer the chopped strawberries to a small bowl, and lightly mash them to release the juices. Add them to the ice cream mixture,\ and stir to completely combine.

Prepare the ice cream according to the ice cream maker instructions. Enjoy immediately like soft-serve, or chill until set.

MINT CHOCOLATE CHIP ICE CREAM

Prep: 30 mins

Cook/Chill: 6 hrs 30 mins

Total: 7 hrs

Yield: 8 servings

Nutritional info per serving:

Carbs	*Fat*	*Protein*
5g	*28g*	*5g*

INGREDIENTS:

2 cans full-fat coconut milk (can size 13.5 - 15 oz)

6 oz fresh mint, with stalks

6 egg yolks

¼ cup MCT oil

3 Tbsp granulated erythritol

2 tsp monk fruit powder

2 tsp vanilla

2 Tbsp toasted cacao nibs

METHOD:

In a medium saucepan, heat the coconut milk over medium heat. Add the mint stalks, and remove the coconut milk from heat. Allow the coconut milk to cool with the mint in it. Set it aside to infuse overnight.

The next day, strain the mint from the coconut milk, squeezing it to release all the flavored coconut milk, and reheat the coconut milk over medium heat.

While the coconut milk is warming, combine the egg yolks, MCT oil, erythritol, and monk fruit in a medium mixing bowl, and whisk to completely combine.

When the coconut milk is steaming but not boiling, remove it from the heat and add it to the egg yolks in a slow, thin, steady stream, whisking constantly. Do not add the milk too quickly or it will scramble the egg yolks.

When the coconut milk and egg yolks are completely combined, return the mixture to the saucepan. Add the vanilla and heat over medium-low. Stir constantly until the mixture thickens, about 20 minutes.

When the mixture is somewhat thick, remove it from the heat and transfer to a clean bowl to cool completely.

Prepare the ice cream according to the ice cream maker instructions. When the ice cream is ready, mix in the cacao nibs.

Enjoy immediately like soft-serve, or chill until set.

SALTED CHOCOLATE ICE CREAM WITH ALMONDS

Prep: 30 mins

Cook/Chill: 6 hrs 30 mins

Total: 7 hrs

Yield: 8 servings

Nutritional info per serving:

Carbs	*Fat*	*Protein*
5g	*28g*	*5g*

INGREDIENTS:

2 cans full-fat coconut milk (can size 13.5 - 15 oz)

6 egg yolks

¼ cup MCT oil

3 Tbsp granulated erythritol

2 tsp monk fruit powder

2 tsp vanilla

6 Tbsp cocoa powder

½ tsp salt

⅓ cup chopped toasted almonds (to mix in)

METHOD:

In a medium saucepan, heat the coconut milk over medium heat.

While the coconut milk is warming, combine the egg yolks, MCT oil, erythritol, cocoa powder, and monk fruit in a medium mixing bowl, and whisk to completely combine.

When the coconut milk is steaming but not boiling, remove it from the heat and add it to the egg yolks in a slow, thin, steady stream, whisking constantly. Do not add the milk too quickly or it will scramble the egg yolks.

When the coconut milk and egg yolks are completely combined, return the mixture to the saucepan. Add the vanilla and salt and heat over medium-low. Stir constantly until the mixture thickens, about 20 minutes.

When the mixture is somewhat thick, remove it from the heat and transfer to a clean bowl to cool completely.

Prepare the ice cream according to the ice cream maker instructions. When the ice cream is done churning, add the chopped almonds, and mix to incorporate.

Enjoy immediately like soft-serve, or freeze until set.

CHAI ICE CREAM

Prep: 30 mins

Cook/Chill: 6 hrs 30 mins

Total: 7 hrs

Yield: 8 servings

Nutritional info per serving:

Carbs	Fat	Protein
3g	27g	4g

INGREDIENTS:

2 cans full-fat coconut milk (can size 13.5 - 15 oz)

6 egg yolks

¼ cup MCT oil

3 Tbsp granulated erythritol

2 tsp monk fruit powder

2 tsp vanilla

Spices:

1 tsp cinnamon

2 tsp powdered ginger

¼ tsp black pepper

½ tsp powdered cardamom

6 bags of black tea (decaffeinated works well too)

METHOD:

In a medium saucepan, heat the coconut milk over medium heat. Add the tea bags and spices, and steep for 1 hour.

When the milk is done steeping, remove the tea bags and return it to the heat to rewarm it.

While the coconut milk is warming, combine the egg yolks, spices, MCT oil, erythritol, and monk fruit in a medium mixing bowl and whisk to completely combine.

When the coconut milk is steaming but not boiling, remove it from the heat, and add it to the egg yolks in a slow, thin, steady stream, whisking constantly to "temper" the egg yolks. Do not add the milk too quickly or it will scramble the egg yolks.

When the coconut milk and egg yolks are completely combined, return the mixture to the saucepan. Add the vanilla and heat over medium-low. Stir constantly until the mixture thickens, about 20 minutes.

When the mixture is somewhat thick, remove it from the heat and transfer to a clean bowl to cool completely.

Prepare the ice cream according to the ice cream maker instructions. Enjoy immediately like soft-serve, or chill until set.

AVOCADO ICE CREAM

Prep: 30 mins

Chill: 6 hrs 30 mins

Total: 7 hrs

Yield: 8 servings

Nutritional info per serving:

Carbs	Fat	Protein
10g	14g	2g

INGREDIENTS:

1½ large ripe avocados

1½ cups coconut cream

4 Tbsp lemon juice

3 tsp monk fruit powder

4 Tbsp powdered erythritol

METHOD:

Combine all ingredients in a high-powered blender. Blend on high until smooth and creamy.

Transfer the avocado mixture to a container, and freeze until solid.

Allow ice cream to sit out 5-10 minutes to soften before scooping and serving.

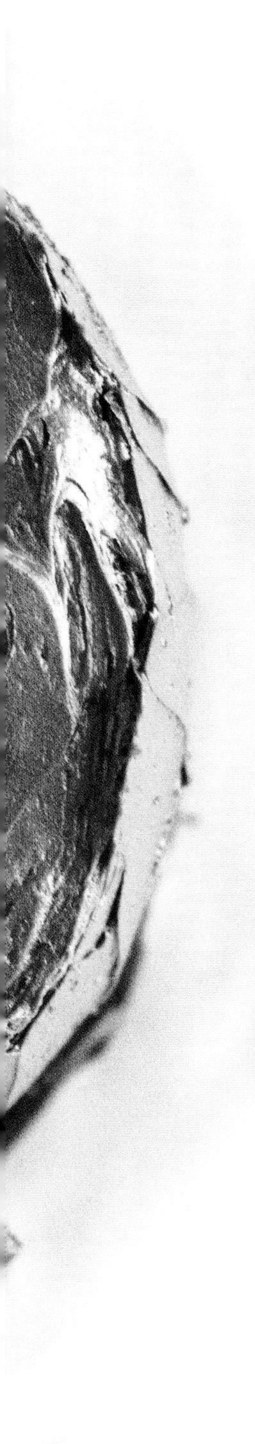

cake

Vanilla Birthday Cake
Classic Chocolate Cake
Matcha Green Tea Cake
Butter Pecan Cake
Spiced Carrot Cake
Chocolate Chip Cookie Cake
Coconut Cake
Mini Chocolate Lava Cakes

VANILLA BIRTHDAY CAKE

Prep: 10 mins

Cook: 45 mins

Total: 55 mins

Yield: 16 servings

Nutrition for 1 slice of 16:

Carbs	*Fat*	*Protein*
4g	*18g*	*4g*

INGREDIENTS:

5 eggs

1¼ cups melted ghee or coconut oil

2 cups full-fat coconut milk

½ cup granulated erythritol

1 Tbsp vanilla

2¼ cups almond flour

¾ cup coconut flour

2 tsp baking soda

2 tsp monk fruit powder

½ tsp salt

METHOD:

Preheat the oven to 350°F. Oil two 8-inch cake pans, line the bottom with parchment paper, and set aside.

In a large mixing bowl, combine the eggs, ghee or oil, coconut milk, erythritol, and vanilla. Whisk until completely combined.

In a medium bowl, combine the almond flour, coconut flour, baking soda, monk fruit, and salt. Whisk to combine.

Add the flour mixture to the egg mixture and mix until a smooth batter is formed.

Evenly distribute the batter between the two prepared cake pans.

Bake 45-50 minutes, until the cake is set in the middle and a toothpick inserted in the middle comes out clean.

When the cakes are done baking, remove them from the oven, and allow them to cool five minutes in the pan. Then remove them from the pan, and allow them to cool completely on a wire cooling rack.

Frost the cake as you wish (the chocolate buttercream is delicious with the vanilla cake), and enjoy!

CLASSIC CHOCOLATE CAKE

Prep: 10 mins

Cook: 45 mins

Total: 55 mins

Yield: 16 servings

Nutrition for 1 slice of 16:

Carbs	*Fat*	*Protein*
4g	*18g*	*5g*

INGREDIENTS:

5 eggs

1¼ cups melted ghee or coconut oil

2 cups full-fat coconut milk

½ cup granulated erythritol

1 Tbsp vanilla

2¼ cups almond flour

¾ cup coconut flour

½ cup cocoa powder

2 tsp baking soda

2 tsp monk fruit powder

½ tsp salt

METHOD:

Preheat the oven to 350°F. Oil two 8-inch cake pans, line the bottom with parchment paper, and set aside.

In a large mixing bowl, combine the eggs, ghee or oil, coconut milk, erythritol, and vanilla. Whisk until completely combined.

In a medium bowl, combine the almond flour, coconut flour, cocoa powder, baking soda, monk fruit, and salt. Whisk to combine.

Add the flour mixture to the egg mixture and mix until a smooth batter is formed.

Evenly distribute the batter between the two prepared cake pans.

Bake 45-50 minutes, until the cake is set in the middle and a toothpick inserted in the middle comes out clean.

When the cakes are done baking, remove them from the oven, and allow them to cool five minutes in the pan. Then remove them from the pan, and allow them to cool completely on a wire cooling rack.

Frost the cake as you wish (the vanilla whipped frosting is yummy), and enjoy!

MATCHA GREEN TEA CAKE

Prep: 10 mins

Cook: 45 mins

Total: 55 mins

Yield: 16 servings

Nutrition for 1 slice of 16:

Carbs	*Fat*	*Protein*
3g	*19g*	*4g*

INGREDIENTS:

5 eggs

1¼ cups melted ghee or coconut oil

2 cups coconut milk

½ cup granulated erythritol

1 Tbsp vanilla

2¼ cups almond flour

¾ cup coconut flour

2½ Tbsp matcha green tea powder

2 tsp baking soda

2 tsp monk fruit powder

½ tsp salt

METHOD:

Preheat the oven to 350°F. Oil two 8-inch cake pans, line the bottom with parchment paper, and set aside.

In a large mixing bowl, combine the eggs, ghee or oil, coconut milk, erythritol, and vanilla. Whisk until completely combined.

In a medium bowl, combine the almond flour, coconut flour, matcha green tea powder, baking soda, monk fruit, and salt. Whisk to combine.

Add the flour mixture to the egg mixture and mix until a smooth batter is formed.

Evenly distribute the batter between the two prepared cake pans.

Bake 45-50 minutes, until the cake is set in the middle and a toothpick inserted in the middle comes out clean.

When the cakes are done baking, remove them from the oven, and allow them to cool five minutes in the pan. Then remove them from the pan, and allow them to cool completely on a wire cooling rack.

Frost the cake as you wish (the lemon whipped frosting works well with this cake), and enjoy!

BUTTER PECAN CAKE

Prep: 20 mins

Cook: 45 mins

Total: 65 mins

Yield: 16 servings

Nutrition for 1 slice of 16:

Carbs	*Fat*	*Protein*
4g	*37g*	*5g*

INGREDIENTS:

5 eggs

1¼ cups melted ghee or butter

2 cups full-fat coconut milk

½ cup granulated erythritol

1½ Tbsp vanilla

2¼ cups almond flour

¾ cup coconut flour

2 tsp baking soda

2 tsp monk fruit powder

½ tsp salt

1 cup chopped pecans, toasted

METHOD:

Preheat the oven to 350°F. Oil two 8-inch cake pans, line the bottom with parchment paper, and set aside.

In a large mixing bowl, combine the eggs, ghee or butter, coconut milk, erythritol, and vanilla. Whisk until completely combined.

In a medium bowl, combine the almond flour, coconut flour, baking soda, monk fruit, and salt. Whisk to combine.

Add the flour mixture to the egg mixture and mix until a smooth batter is formed. Mix the chopped pecans into the batter.

Evenly distribute the batter between the two prepared cake pans.

Bake 45-50 minutes, until the cake is set in the middle and a toothpick inserted in the middle comes out clean.

When the cakes are done baking, remove them from the oven, and allow them to cool five minutes in the pan. Then remove them from the pan and allow them to cool completely on a wire cooling rack.

Frost the cake as you wish (the vanilla buttercream frosting is great with this cake), and enjoy!

SPICED CARROT CAKE

Prep: 20 mins

Cook: 45 mins

Total: 65 mins

Yield: 16 servings

Nutrition for 1 slice of 16:

Carbs	Fat	Protein
3g	18g	4g

INGREDIENTS:

5 eggs

1 cups melted ghee or coconut oil

2 cups full-fat coconut milk

½ cup granulated erythritol

2 tsp vanilla

2¼ cups almond flour

¾ cup coconut flour

2 tsp cinnamon

¼ tsp nutmeg

¼ tsp cardamom

½ tsp ground ginger

2 tsp baking soda

2 tsp monk fruit powder

½ tsp salt

1 tsp fresh grated orange zest, optional

To fold in:

½ cup grated carrots

½ cup chopped toasted walnuts

METHOD:

Preheat the oven to 350°F. Oil two 8-inch cake pans, line the bottom with parchment paper, and set aside.

In a large mixing bowl, combine the eggs, ghee or oil, coconut milk, erythritol, and vanilla. Whisk until completely combined.

In a medium bowl, combine the almond flour, coconut flour, spices, baking soda, monk fruit, and salt. Whisk to combine.

Add the flour mixture to the egg mixture, and mix until a smooth batter is formed.

Fold in the shredded carrots and toasted walnuts, and mix to evenly combine.

Evenly distribute the batter between the two prepared cake pans.

Bake 45-50 minutes, until the cake is set in the middle and a toothpick inserted in the middle comes out clean.

When the cakes are done baking, remove them from the oven, and allow them to cool five minutes in the pan. Then remove them from the pan and allow them to cool completely on a wire cooling rack.

Frost the cake as you wish (the vanilla buttercream frosting is great with this), and enjoy!

CHOCOLATE CHIP COOKIE CAKE

Prep: 10 mins

Cook: 25 mins

Total: 35 mins

Yield: 16 servings

Nutrition for 1 slice of 16:

Carbs	Fat	Protein
0g	6g	1g

INGREDIENTS:

2 cups almond flour

⅓ cup granulated erythritol

2 tsp monk fruit powder

¼ tsp sea salt

1 egg

½ cup melted coconut oil or ghee

2 tsp vanilla

2 Tbsp cacao nibs

METHOD:

Preheat the oven to 350°F. Oil one 8-inch cake pan, line the bottom with parchment paper, and set aside.

In a large mixing bowl, combine the almond flour, erythritol, monk fruit, and sea salt. Whisk until completely combined.

In a medium bowl, combine the egg, coconut oil or ghee, and vanilla. Whisk to combine.

Add the egg mixture to the almond flour mixture, and mix until a smooth, thick batter is formed.

Fold in the cacao nibs until they are incorporated.

Evenly press the batter into the prepared cake pan.

Bake 25-30 minutes, until the cake is set in the middle and a toothpick inserted in the middle comes out clean.

When the cake is done baking, remove it from the oven, and allow it to cool five minutes in the pan. Then remove it from the pan, and allow it to cool completely on a wire cooling rack.

Frost the cake as you wish, or enjoy it as is!

COCONUT CAKE

Prep: 10 mins

Cook: 45 mins

Total: 55 mins

Yield: 16 servings

Nutrition for 1 slice of 16:

Carbs	Fat	Protein
3g	30g	4g

INGREDIENTS:

5 eggs

1¼ cups melted coconut oil

2 cups full-fat coconut milk

½ cup granulated erythritol

2 tsp vanilla

2¼ cups almond flour

¾ cup coconut flour

1 cup shredded coconut

2 tsp baking soda

2 tsp monk fruit powder

½ tsp salt

METHOD:

Preheat the oven to 350°F. Oil two 8-inch cake pans, line the bottom with parchment paper, and set aside.

In a large mixing bowl, combine the eggs, coconut oil, coconut milk, erythritol, and vanilla. Whisk until completely combined.

In a medium bowl, combine the almond flour, coconut flour, shredded coconut, baking soda, monk fruit, and salt. Whisk to combine.

Add the flour mixture to the egg mixture, and mix until a smooth batter is formed.

Evenly distribute the batter between the two prepared cake pans.

Bake 45-50 minutes, until the cake is set in the middle and a toothpick inserted in the middle comes out clean.

When the cakes are done baking, remove them from the oven and allow them to cool five minutes in the pan. Then remove them from the pan and allow them to cool completely on a wire cooling rack.

Frost the cake with vanilla whipped cream frosting, and enjoy!

MINI CHOCOLATE LAVA CAKES

Prep: 10 mins

Cook: 10 mins

Total: 20 mins

Yield: 8 servings

Nutrition for 1 piece:

Carbs	Fat	Protein
1g	2g	2g

INGREDIENTS:

½ cup cacao powder

¼ cup granulated erythritol

1 tsp monk fruit powder

¼ tsp salt

1 tsp baking powder

4 eggs

¼ cup full-fat coconut milk

1 tsp vanilla

METHOD:

Preheat the oven to 350°F. Line a muffin tin with parchment paper. Alternatively, you can use an oiled silicone muffin tin. Set aside.

In a medium bowl, add the cacao powder, erythritol, monk fruit, salt, and baking powder. Mix to combine.

In a separate small bowl, combine the eggs, coconut milk, and vanilla. Mix well.

Add the egg mixture to the cacao powder mixture, and mix until a smooth batter is formed.

Pour into the prepared muffin tins.

Bake for 10-15 minutes, until the top is barely set and still jiggly.

Allow the cakes to cool until they can be handled, then turn them out of the tins.

Serve warm, and enjoy!

frosting

German Chocolate Cake Frosting
Chocolate Whipped Cream Frosting
Lemon Whipped Cream Frosting
Vanilla Whipped Cream Frosting
Vanilla Buttercream Frosting
Chocolate Buttercream Frosting
Cream Cheese Frosting

GERMAN CHOCOLATE CAKE FROSTING

Prep: 10 mins

Cook: 15 mins

Total: 25 mins

Yield: 16 servings

Nutrition for 1 slice of 16:

Carbs	Fat	Protein
2g	18g	2g

INGREDIENTS:

4 large eggs yolks

¼ cup melted coconut oil

¼ cup melted palm shortening

¼ cup erythritol

½ cup full-fat coconut milk

1 tsp vanilla

1 cup chopped pecans

½ tsp monk fruit powder

⅛ tsp sea salt

1⅓ cups shredded coconut

METHOD:

In a medium saucepan, combine eggs yolks, oil, shortening, erythritol, and coconut milk. Heat to a light simmer, stirring constantly. *Note: Make sure you keep stirring! If you stop, you will get scrambled eggs!*

When the mixture begins to simmer, remove the pot from the heat and transfer the contents to a medium bowl. Add vanilla, pecans, monk fruit extract, salt, and coconut, and mix well.

Set aside to cool completely before using.

CHOCOLATE WHIPPED CREAM FROSTING

Prep: 15 mins

Chill: 4 hrs 30 mins

Total: 4 hrs 45 mins

Yield: 16 servings

Nutrition for 1 slice of 16:

Carbs	Fat	Protein
1g	9g	2g

INGREDIENTS:

¼ cup cool water

1 Tbsp gelatin

¼ cup boiling water

2 cups coconut cream

½ cup cacao powder

2 tsp vanilla extract

1½ tsp monk fruit powder

2 Tbsp powdered erythritol

METHOD:

In a small bowl, pour the ¼ cup cool water. Sprinkle the gelatin over the water, and whisk it in to allow it to hydrate and soak up all the water.

When the gelatin is absorbed, add the boiling water to the gelatin and stir to dissolve.

Combine all ingredients in a high-powered blender, and blend until smooth.

Refrigerate for 4 hours or overnight to set.

Whip the frosting on a high speed with an electric mixer before using.

LEMON WHIPPED CREAM FROSTING

Prep: 15 mins

Chill: 4 hrs 30 mins

Total: 4 hrs 45 mins

Yield: 16 servings

Nutrition for 1 slice of 16:

Carbs	Fat	Protein
2g	6g	1g

INGREDIENTS:

⅓ cup fresh lemon juice

1 Tbsp gelatin

⅓ cup boiling water

2 cups coconut cream

1 tsp lemon zest

1 tsp vanilla extract

1½ tsp monk fruit powder

2 Tbsp powdered erythritol

METHOD:

In a small bowl, pour the ⅓ cup lemon juice. Sprinkle the gelatin over the lemon juice, and allow it to hydrate and soak up all the water.

Pour the boiling water over the gelatin, and stir to dissolve.

Combine all ingredients in a high-powered blender, and blend until smooth.

Refrigerate for four hours or overnight to set.

Whip the frosting on high speed with an electric mixer before using.

VANILLA WHIPPED CREAM FROSTING

Prep: 15 mins

Chill: 4 hrs 30 mins

Total: 4 hrs 45 mins

Yield: 16 servings

Nutrition for 1 slice of 16:

Carbs	Fat	Protein
2g	6g	1g

INGREDIENTS:

4 Tbsp cool water

1 Tbsp gelatin

⅓ cup boiling water

2 cups coconut cream

2 tsp vanilla extract

1½ tsp monk fruit powder

2 Tbsp powdered erythritol

METHOD:

In a small bowl, pour the 4 tablespoons cool water. Sprinkle the gelatin over the water, and whisk it in to allow it to hydrate and soak up all the water.

When the gelatin is absorbed, add the boiling water to the gelatin, and stir to dissolve.

Combine all ingredients in a high-powered blender and blend until smooth.

Refrigerate for 4 hours or overnight to set.

Whip the frosting on high speed with an electric mixer before using.

VANILLA BUTTERCREAM FROSTING

Prep: 5 mins

Chill: 5 mins

Total: 10 mins

Yield: 16 servings

Nutrition for 1 slice of 16:

Carbs	Fat	Protein
9g	24g	0g

INGREDIENTS:

2 cups butter, softened

2 cups powdered Zsweet erythritol sweetener, sifted

¾ tsp monk fruit powder

1 Tbsp vanilla

6 Tbsp full-fat coconut milk

METHOD:

Combine all ingredients except coconut milk in a large mixing bowl.

With an electric mixer, mash the ingredients together to begin to combine them, then whip on high until they are combined.

Add the coconut milk and continue whipping until a smooth texture is achieved.

Store in the fridge up to five days.

CHOCOLATE BUTTERCREAM FROSTING

Prep: 5 mins

Chill: 5 mins

Total: 10 mins

Yield: 16 servings

Nutrition for 1 slice of 16:

Carbs	*Fat*	*Protein*
1g	*24g*	*1g*

INGREDIENTS:

2 cups butter, softened

2 cups powdered Zsweet erythritol sweetener, sifted

½ tsp monk fruit powder

2 tsp vanilla

6 Tbsp cacao powder, sifted

6 Tbsp full-fat coconut milk

METHOD:

Combine all ingredients except coconut milk in a large mixing bowl.

With an electric mixer, mash the ingredients together to begin to combine them, then whip on high until they are combined.

Add the coconut milk and continue whipping until a smooth texture is achieved.

Store in the fridge up to five days.

CREAM CHEESE FROSTING

Prep: 10 mins

Chill: 4 hrs

Total: 4 hrs 10 mins

Yield: 16 servings

Nutrition for 1 slice of 16:

Carbs	Fat	Protein
3g	16g	2g

INGREDIENTS:

4 Tbsp cool water

1½ Tbsp gelatin

½ cup boiling water

2 cups macadamia nuts, soaked for eight hours or overnight

1 cup coconut cream

½ cup powdered erythritol

2 tsp monk fruit powder

⅓ cup lemon juice

1 tsp apple cider vinegar

2 tsp vanilla

METHOD:

In a small bowl, pour the 4 tablespoons cool water. Sprinkle the gelatin over the water, and whisk it in to allow it to hydrate and soak up all the water.

When the gelatin is absorbed, add the boiling water to the gelatin, and stir to dissolve.

Combine all ingredients in a high-powered blender, and blend until smooth.

Refrigerate for four hours or overnight to set.

Whip the frosting on high speed with an electric mixer before using. ***Note: Allow the frosting to sit out for 10-15 minutes to warm up slightly before using so that it will be easier to spread.***

brownies

Walnut Brownies
Almond Butter Brownie Bites
Congo Bar Blondie Brownies
Pecan Butter Swirl Brownies
Mint Brownies
Mexican Hot Chocolate Brownies

WALNUT BROWNIES

Prep: 15 mins

Cook: 30 mins

Total: 45 mins

Yield: 16 brownies

Nutrition per Brownie:

Carbs	*Fat*	*Protein*
3g	*9g*	*3g*

INGREDIENTS:

¼ cup melted coconut oil or ghee

¼ cup full-fat coconut milk

⅔ cup cacao powder

3 eggs

1 tsp vanilla

⅓ cup granulated erythritol

1 cup almond flour

½ tsp sea salt

2 tsp pure monk fruit powder

⅓ cup chopped toasted walnuts + 2 Tbsp (to garnish)

METHOD:

Preheat the oven to 350°F. Line an 8-inch x 8-inch baking dish with parchment paper, and set aside.

In a medium bowl, mix the coconut oil, coconut milk, cacao powder, eggs, vanilla, and erythritol until completely combined.

In a small bowl, mix the almond flour, salt, and monk fruit powder.

Combine the egg mixture and the almond flour mixture. Mix to form a smooth batter. Fold in the walnuts until evenly incorporated.

Transfer the batter to the prepared baking dish, and smooth it out to fill the baking dish evenly. Sprinkle the remaining walnuts over the batter, and lightly press them in.

Bake for 30-35 minutes, until the brownies are set and a toothpick inserted in the center comes out clean.

Allow the brownies to cool completely in the pan before cutting and serving.

ALMOND BUTTER BROWNIE BITES

Prep: 10 mins

Cook: 30 mins

Total: 40 mins

Yield: 16 brownie bites

Nutrition per Brownie:

Carbs	*Fat*	*Protein*
2g	*10g*	*4g*

INGREDIENTS:

1 cup creamy almond butter

¾ cup full-fat coconut milk

1 tsp monk fruit powder

⅓ cup granulated erythritol

1 Tbsp vanilla

¼ tsp salt

1 tsp baking powder

METHOD:

Preheat the oven to 325°F. Line an 8-inch x 8-inch glass baking dish with parchment paper, and set it aside.

Combine the almond butter, coconut milk, monk fruit, erythritol, vanilla, and salt in a medium mixing bowl. Mix until a smooth batter is formed.

Add the baking powder, and mix well to evenly distribute it throughout the batter.

Spread the batter into the prepared baking dish.

Bake for 30-35 minutes, until the center is set and a toothpick inserted in the middle comes out mostly clean.

Allow the brownies to cool completely before slicing.

CONGO BAR BLONDIE BROWNIES

Prep: 10 mins

Cook: 30 mins

Total: 40 mins

Yield: 16 brownie

Nutrition per Brownie:

Carbs	Fat	Protein
2g	11g	4g

INGREDIENTS:

1 cup creamy almond butter

½ cup full-fat coconut milk

1 tsp monk fruit powder

⅓ cup granulated erythritol

1 Tbsp vanilla

¼ tsp salt

1 tsp baking powder

2 Tbsp coconut flour

⅓ cup coconut flakes + 2 Tbsp (to garnish)

2 Tbsp cacao nibs + 1 Tbsp (to garnish)

METHOD:

Preheat the oven to 325°F. Line an 8-inch x 8-inch glass baking dish with parchment paper, and set it aside.

Combine the almond butter, coconut milk, monk fruit, erythritol, vanilla, and salt in a medium mixing bowl. Mix until a smooth batter is formed.

Add the baking powder and coconut flour, and mix well to evenly distribute it throughout the batter.

Fold in ⅓ cup coconut flakes and 2 tablespoons cacao nibs until evenly distributed throughout the batter.

Spread the batter into the prepared baking dish. Sprinkle with remaining coconut and cacao nibs.

Bake for 30-35 minutes, until the center is set and a toothpick inserted in the middle comes out mostly clean.

Allow the brownies to cool completely before slicing.

PECAN BUTTER SWIRL BROWNIES

Prep: 15 mins

Cook: 30 mins

Total: 45 mins

Yield: 16 brownies

Nutrition per Brownie:

Carbs	Fat	Protein
2g	9g	3g

INGREDIENTS:

¼ cup melted coconut oil or ghee

¼ cup full-fat coconut milk

⅔ cup cacao powder

3 eggs

1 tsp vanilla

⅓ cup granulated erythritol

1 cup almond flour

½ tsp sea salt

2 tsp pure monk fruit powder

⅓ cup pecan butter (to swirl in)

METHOD:

Preheat the oven to 350°F. Line an 8-inch x 8-inch baking dish with parchment paper, and set aside.

In a medium bowl, mix the coconut oil, coconut milk, cacao powder, eggs, vanilla, and erythritol until completely combined.

In a small bowl, mix the almond flour, salt, and monk fruit powder.

Combine the egg mixture and the almond flour mixture, and mix to form a smooth batter.

Transfer the batter to the prepared baking dish. and smooth it out to fill the baking dish evenly.

Drizzle the pecan butter over the brownie batter, and drag a knife across the drizzles (in the opposite direction) three to four times to swirl the pecan butter in.

Bake for 30-35 minutes, until the brownies are set and a toothpick inserted in the center comes out clean.

Allow the brownies to cool completely in the pan before cutting and serving.

MINT BROWNIES

Prep: 25 mins

Cook: 35 mins

Total: 1 hour

Yield: 16 brownies

Nutrition per Brownie with frosting:

Carbs	*Fat*	*Protein*
2g	*18g*	*2g*

INGREDIENTS:

¼ cup melted coconut oil or ghee

¼ cup coconut milk

⅔ cup cacao powder

3 eggs

1 tsp vanilla

⅓ cup granulated erythritol

1 cup almond flour

½ tsp sea salt

2 tsp pure monk fruit powder

Mint Frosting Layer:

½ cup palm shortening, softened

½ cup butter, softened

½ cup powdered erythritol, sifted

¾ tsp monk fruit powder

15 drops peppermint essential oil (food-grade)

Chlorophyll 30 drops for color, optional

METHOD:

To Prepare the Brownies:

Preheat the oven to 350°F. Line an 8-inch x 8-inch baking dish with parchment paper, and set aside.

In a medium bowl, mix the coconut oil, coconut milk, cacao powder, eggs, vanilla, and erythritol until completely combined.

In a small bowl, mix the almond flour, salt, and monk fruit extract.

Combine the egg mixture and the almond flour mixture, and mix to form a smooth batter. Fold in the walnuts until evenly incorporated.

Transfer the batter to the prepared baking dish and smooth it out to fill the baking dish evenly.

Bake for 30-35 minutes, until the brownies are set and a toothpick inserted in the center comes out clean.

Allow the brownies to cool completely in the pan before frosting.

To Prepare the Frosting:

While the brownies are baking, combine the palm shortening, butter, powdered erythritol, and monk fruit in a large mixing bowl.

Use the electric mixer to mash the ingredients together before turning on the beaters (this will prevent a major cloud of erythritol from erupting in your face). Then whip until smooth and creamy.

Add the peppermint essential oil and optional chlorophyll and whip until a uniform peppermint flavor and green color are achieved.

When the brownies are cool, spread the frosting evenly over the brownies.

Serve immediately, or chill the frosted brownies 30 minutes to 1 hour to set the frosting for a cleaner slice.

MEXICAN HOT CHOCOLATE BROWNIES

Prep: 10 mins

Cook: 30 mins

Total: 40 mins

Yield: 16 brownies

Nutr. per Brownie with cacao nibs:

Carbs	Fat	Protein
2g	8g	3g

INGREDIENTS:

½ cup cacao nibs, divided (optional)

¼ cup melted coconut oil or ghee

¼ cup coconut milk

⅔ cup cacao powder

3 eggs

1 tsp vanilla

⅓ cup granulated erythritol

1 cup almond flour

½ tsp sea salt

2 tsp cinnamon

¼ tsp cayenne

½ tsp ancho chili powder

¼ tsp nutmeg

¼ tsp ground coffee or espresso

2 tsp pure monk fruit powder

METHOD:

Preheat the oven to 350°F. Line an 8-inch x 8-inch baking dish with parchment paper, and set aside.

Spread the cacao nibs on a baking sheet and toast them for 7-10 minutes, until the oils are released (you can tell when this happens because the nibs get shiny). Set aside to cool.

In a medium bowl, mix the coconut oil, coconut milk, cacao powder, eggs, vanilla, and erythritol until completely combined.

In a small bowl, mix the almond flour, salt, spices, ground coffee, and monk fruit extract.

Combine the egg mixture and the almond flour mixture, and mix to form a smooth batter. Fold in ⅓ cup of the cacao nibs until evenly incorporated.

Transfer the batter to the prepared baking dish, and smooth it out to fill the baking dish evenly. Sprinkle the remaining cacao nibs over the batter, and lightly press them in.

Bake for 30-35 minutes, until the brownies are set and a toothpick inserted in the center comes out clean.

Allow the brownies to cool completely in the pan before cutting and serving.

candy

Chocolate Chip Cookie Dough Bites
Peppermint Patties
Almond Butter Cups
Chocolate Covered Bacon Bites
Chocolate Bark
Raspberry Chocolate Bark
Salted Almond Chocolate Bark
White Chocolate Bark
White Chocolate Walnut Butter Cups
Chocolate Covered Coconut Mound Bars
Matcha Pistachio Fat Bombs
Strawberry Cashew Fat Bombs
Easy Chocolate Truffles
Dark Chocolate Covered Key Lime Truffles

CHOCOLATE CHIP COOKIE DOUGH BITES

Prep: 10 mins

Cook/Chill: 1 hr 15 mins

Total: 1 hr 25 mins

Yield: 24-30 bites

Nutrition for 2 from a yield of 30: (with chocolate coating)

Carbs	Fat	Protein
4g	16g	3g

INGREDIENTS:

2 cups raw cashews

1 tsp monk fruit powder

3 Tbsp melted coconut oil

1 tsp vanilla extract

¼ tsp salt

2 Tbsp cacao nibs

Chocolate Coating

2 oz unsweetened baking chocolate

2 oz cacao butter

¼ + ⅛ tsp monk fruit powder

METHOD:

To Prepare the Cookie Dough Bites:

Process the cashews and the monk fruit powder in a food processor fitted with an "S" blade until a fine powder forms.

Add the coconut oil, vanilla extract, and salt, and process until a dough forms.

Transfer the cookie dough to a bowl, and mix in the cacao nibs.

Scoop the cookie dough by the tablespoonful, and form into balls with your hands.

Place the cookie dough balls on a parchment-lined baking sheet, and pop them in the fridge for 30 minutes to set.

While the Cookie Dough Sets, Prepare the Chocolate Coating:

Combine all coating ingredients in the bowl of a double boiler.

Heat over medium until the mixture is mostly melted. Remove it from the heat, and allow it to continue melting, mixing occasionally.

Allow the chocolate to cool a bit so it thickens slightly (this will create a thicker chocolate coat on the cookie dough balls).

When you're ready to coat the cookie dough balls, remove them from the fridge. Drop them one at a time into the chocolate. Use a fork to roll them around to coat them, then transfer them back to the parchment-lined baking sheet.

Return them to the fridge to set the chocolate coating, 30 minutes to 1 hour. Store in an airtight container in the fridge for 5-7 days.

PEPPERMINT PATTIES

Prep: 20 mins

Cook/Chill: 45 mins

Total: 1 hr 5 mins

Yield: 12-16 mini cups

Nutrition for 2 from a yield of 16:

Carbs	Fat	Protein
2g	22g	2g

INGREDIENTS:

Peppermint Filling

½ cup coconut butter, softened

1 Tbsp powdered erythritol, sifted

¼ tsp monk fruit powder

8-10 drops peppermint essential oil

Chocolate Coating

3 oz cacao butter

3 oz unsweetened baking chocolate

¼ tsp monk fruit powder

METHOD:

To Prepare the Filling:

Heat the coconut butter in a small saucepan over medium-low heat until it is softened and able to be stirred.

Combine all the filling ingredients in a small bowl and mix to completely combine. Place the bowl in the fridge to set the filling while you make the chocolate coating.

To Prepare the Chocolate Coating:

Combine all ingredients in the bowl of a double boiler.

Heat over medium until the ingredients are mostly melted.

Remove the bowl from the heat, and stir to combine the ingredients, then set aside and allow the chocolate to cool.

To Assemble:

Line a mini muffin tin with parchment paper liners. Set aside.

When the coconut butter mixture is firm enough to scoop, remove it from the fridge.

Scoop ½ teaspoon-size balls and flatten them slightly into disc shapes. Set aside.

Scoop 1 teaspoon of chocolate into the prepared muffin tins. Place one of the flattened peppermint coconut butter discs into each tin, and top with 1 teaspoon of chocolate.

Chill 30 minutes or until set.

Store in the fridge up to two weeks.

ALMOND BUTTER CUPS

Prep: 15 mins

Cook/Chill: 30 mins

Total: 45 mins

Yield: 12-16 mini cups

Nutrition for 2 from a yield of 12:

Carbs	*Fat*	*Protein*
3g	*29g*	*6g*

INGREDIENTS:

Almond Butter Filling

6 Tbsp almond butter

¼ tsp monk fruit powder

¼ tsp salt

½ tsp vanilla

Chocolate Coating

3 oz unsweetened baking chocolate

3 oz cacao butter

¼ tsp monk fruit powder

METHOD:

To Prepare the Filling:

Combine all the filling ingredients in a small bowl, and mix to completely combine. Set the bowl in the fridge to set the filling while you make the chocolate coating.

To Prepare the Chocolate Coating:

Combine all ingredients in the bowl of a double boiler.

Heat over medium until the ingredients are mostly melted.

Remove the bowl from the heat, and stir to combine the ingredients, then set aside and allow the chocolate to cool.

To Assemble:

Line a mini muffin tin with parchment paper liners. Set aside.

When the almond butter mixture is firm enough to scoop, remove it from the fridge.

Scoop ½ teaspoon-size balls and flatten them slightly into disc shapes. Set aside.

Scoop 1 teaspoon of chocolate into the prepared muffin tins. Place one of the flattened almond butter discs into each tin, and top with 1 teaspoon of chocolate.

Chill 30 minutes or until set.

Store in the fridge up to two weeks.

CHOCOLATE COVERED BACON BITES

Prep: 30 mins

Cook/Chill: 30 mins

Total: 1 hour

Yield: 16 bites

Nutrition for 2 from a yield of 16:

Carbs	*Fat*	*Protein*
0g	*14g*	*3g*

INGREDIENTS:

4 strips thick-cut bacon

1 oz cacao paste or unsweetened baking chocolate

3 oz cacao butter

⅛ tsp monk fruit powder

⅛ tsp vanilla powder

METHOD:

To Prepare the Bacon:

Preheat the oven to 400°F. Place a wire cooling rack on top of a baking sheet, and lay the bacon strips on the cooling rack.

Bake the bacon until almost crispy, 25-30 minutes.

Cool and chop each strip into four pieces.

To Prepare the Chocolate Coating:

Line a baking sheet with parchment paper and set aside.

Combine the baking chocolate, cacao butter, monk fruit, and vanilla in the bowl of a double boiler. Heat over medium until the ingredients are melted, then set aside to allow the chocolate to cool slightly (this will allow for a thicker chocolate coating on the bacon).

When the chocolate is slightly thickened, dip each piece of bacon into the chocolate and set it on the prepared parchment-lined baking sheet.

Pop the baking sheet in the fridge, and chill to set the chocolate, 20-30 minutes.

Store in the fridge in an airtight container up to five days.

CHOCOLATE BARK

Prep: 5 mins

Cook/Chill: 40 mins

Total: 45 mins

Yield: 20-30 pieces

Nutrition for 2 from a yield of 20:

Carbs	*Fat*	*Protein*
2g	*26g*	*2g*

INGREDIENTS:

6 oz unsweetened baking chocolate

6 oz cacao butter

2 Tbsp powdered erythritol, sifted

¼ + ⅛ tsp monk fruit powder

¼ tsp vanilla powder

METHOD:

Line a 9-inch x 13-inch baking sheet with parchment paper, and set aside.

Combine all ingredients in the bowl of a double boiler.

Heat over medium until the ingredients are mostly melted.

Remove the bowl from the heat, and whisk to combine the ingredients.

Pour the melted chocolate over the prepared baking sheet, and place it in the fridge to chill until set, 30 minutes or overnight.

When the chocolate is set, break it into pieces and store in an airtight container in the fridge up to two weeks.

RASPBERRY CHOCOLATE BARK

Prep: 5 mins

Cook/Chill: 40 mins

Total: 45 mins

Yield: 20-30 pieces

Nutrition for 2 from a yield of 20:

Carbs	Fat	Protein
2g	26g	2g

INGREDIENTS:

6 oz unsweetened baking chocolate

6 oz cacao butter

2 Tbsp powdered erythritol, sifted

¼ + ⅛ tsp monk fruit powder

¼ tsp vanilla powder

*1 Tbsp powdered freeze dried raspberries**

METHOD:

Line a 9-inch x 13-inch baking sheet with parchment paper, and set aside.

Combine all ingredients in the bowl of a double boiler.

Heat over medium until the ingredients are mostly melted.

Remove the bowl from the heat, and whisk to combine the ingredients.

Pour the melted chocolate over the prepared baking sheet, and sprinkle the powdered raspberries over it evenly.

Place it in the fridge to chill until set, 30 minutes or overnight.

When the chocolate is set, break it into pieces and store in an airtight container in the fridge up to two weeks.

** I buy my freeze-dried raspberries at a store call Trader Joe's—you can also find them online on Amazon.com. To powder the raspberries, simply place 2 tablespoons of freeze-dried berries into a plastic bag and crush them under the heel of your hand until they are close to a powder. Measure this to pour over your chocolate bark for a fruity pop!*

SALTED ALMOND CHOCOLATE BARK

Prep: 5 mins

Cook/Chill: 40 mins

Total: 45 mins

Yield: 20-30 pieces

Nutrition for 2 from a yield of 20:

Carbs	*Fat*	*Protein*
2g	*27g*	*3g*

INGREDIENTS:

6 oz unsweetened baking chocolate

6 oz cacao butter

2 Tbsp powdered erythritol, sifted

¼ + ⅛ tsp monk fruit powder

¼ tsp vanilla powder

¼ - ½ tsp coarse salt, to taste

¼ cup chopped toasted almonds

METHOD:

Line a 9-inch x 13-inch baking sheet with parchment paper, and set aside.

Combine all ingredients in the bowl of a double boiler.

Heat over medium until the ingredients are mostly melted.

Remove the bowl from the heat, and whisk to combine the ingredients.

Pour the melted chocolate over the prepared baking sheet, and sprinkle the salt and almonds evenly over the top.

Place it in the fridge to chill until set, 30 minutes or overnight.

When the chocolate is set, break it into pieces and store in an airtight container in the fridge up to two weeks.

WHITE CHOCOLATE BARK

Prep: 5 mins

Cook/Chill: 40 mins

Total: 45 mins

Yield: 20-30 pieces (equals 1 batch)

Nutrition for 2 from a yield of 20:

Carbs	Fat	Protein
1g	16g	0g

INGREDIENTS:

½ cup coconut butter

4 oz cacao butter

⅛ tsp vanilla powder

1 Tbsp + 2 tsp powdered erythritol, sifted

⅛ tsp monk fruit powder

1 tsp vanilla extract

METHOD:

Line a 9-inch x 13-inch baking sheet with parchment paper, and set aside.

Combine all ingredients in the bowl of a double boiler.

Heat over medium until the ingredients are mostly melted.

Remove the bowl from the heat, and whisk to combine the ingredients.

Pour the melted white chocolate over the prepared baking sheet, and place it in the fridge to chill until set, 30 minutes or overnight.

When the white chocolate is set, break it into pieces, and store in an airtight container in the fridge up to two weeks.

WHITE CHOCOLATE WALNUT BUTTER CUPS

Prep: 15 mins

Cook/Chill: 40 mins

Total: 55 mins

Yield: 24-36 mini cups

Nutrition for 2 from a yield of 24:

Carbs	*Fat*	*Protein*
1g	*16g*	*1g*

INGREDIENTS:

½ cup walnuts

1 batch White Chocolate Bark (recipe page 91)

METHOD:

To Prepare the Walnut Butter:

Preheat the oven to 350°F.

Spread ½ cup walnuts over a baking sheet, and roast them for 10 minutes.

After 10 minutes, remove the walnuts from the oven, and transfer them immediately to the bowl of a food processor fitted with an "S" blade and process into a paste. Set aside.

To Prepare the White Chocolate Coating:

Combine all ingredients for the White Chocolate Bark in the bowl of a double boiler.

Heat over medium until the ingredients are melted.

Remove the bowl from the heat, and stir to combine the ingredients, then set aside and allow the white chocolate to cool.

To Assemble:

Line a mini muffin tin with parchment paper liners.

Scoop 1 teaspoon of white chocolate into the prepared muffin tins. Scoop ½ teaspoon of walnut butter into the muffin tin and top with 1 teaspoon of white chocolate.

Chill 30 minutes or until set.

Store in the fridge up to two weeks.

CHOCOLATE COVERED COCONUT MOUND BARS

Prep: 15 mins

Cook/Chill: 1 hr 35 mins

Total: 1 hr 50 mins

Yield: 10-12 bars

Nutrition for 1 from a yield of 10:

Carbs	*Fat*	*Protein*
3g	*36g*	*2g*

INGREDIENTS:

3 cups shredded coconut

½ cup coconut oil

½ cup coconut cream

½ tsp monk fruit powder

3 Tbsp powdered erythritol

½ tsp vanilla

Chocolate Coating

1 oz unsweetened baking chocolate

3 oz cacao butter

¼ tsp monk fruit powder

Note: Toast coconut five minutes at 350°F in the oven.

METHOD:

To Prepare the Filling:

Line an 8-inch x 8-inch baking dish with parchment paper, and set aside.

In a food processor fitted with an "S" blade, blend all filling ingredients until smooth.

Scoop the filling into the prepared baking dish and press it to fit evenly.

Chill the filling until solid, one hour or overnight.

To Prepare the Coating:

Melt chocolate ingredients together in double boiler.

Allow the chocolate to cool until just warm to the touch.

To Assemble the Bars:

Line a baking sheet with parchment paper, and set it aside.

When the filling is set, remove it from the fridge, and remove the filling from the baking dish, leaving it on the parchment paper. Use a sharp knife to cut the filling in half, then into 10-12 bars.

Transfer the chocolate to a medium bowl with a wide base.

Dip the bars in the chocolate and cover them, using a spoon to scoop chocolate over them to cover them completely. Lay the bars on the prepared baking sheet as they are covered.

Chill the bars in the fridge until chocolate is set, 20 minutes or so. Store in the fridge up to two weeks.

MATCHA PISTACHIO FAT BOMBS

Prep: 15 mins

Chill: 40 mins

Total: 55 mins

Yield: 12 fat bombs

Nutrition for 1 Fat Bomb:

Carbs	Fat	Protein
5g	14g	3g

INGREDIENTS:

1 cup coconut butter

½ cup cashew butter

1½ tsp matcha powder

½ tsp monk fruit powder

¼ cup pistachio meats

METHOD:

Combine the coconut butter, cashew butter, matcha powder, and monk fruit in the bowl of a food processor fitted with an "S" blade.

Process until the batter is smooth and everything is mixed in.

Transfer the batter to a small bowl, and mix in pistachios. Spoon into a silicone candy mold or lined muffin tin, and chill until solid.

Store in an airtight container in the fridge up to two weeks.

STRAWBERRY CASHEW FAT BOMBS

Prep: 15 mins

Chill: 40 mins

Total: 55 mins

Yield: 12 fat bombs

Nutrition for 1 Fat Bomb:

Carbs	Fat	Protein
4g	12g	3g

INGREDIENTS:

6 g freeze-dried strawberries (about ¼ cup)

½ cup cashew butter

1 cup coconut butter

½ tsp monk fruit powder, to taste

1 Tbsp lemon juice

½ tsp vanilla extract

METHOD:

Combine all the ingredients in the bowl of a food processor fitted with an "S" blade.

Process until the batter is smooth and everything is mixed in.

Grab 2 silicone ice cube molds, and use a tablespoon to fill the individual cavities.

Freeze for 4 hours or until solid.

Store in an airtight container in the fridge for up to two weeks.

EASY CHOCOLATE TRUFFLES

Prep: 20 mins

Cook/Chill: 1 hour

Total: 1 hr 20 mins

Yield: 16 truffles

Nutrition for 2 from yield of 16: (includes chocolate coating)

Carbs	*Fat*	*Protein*
3g	*28g*	*6g*

INGREDIENTS:

¾ cup almond butter or other nut butter

¼ cup coconut cream

¼ + ⅛ tsp monk fruit powder

¼ tsp salt

½ tsp vanilla

3 Tbsp cacao powder

Chocolate Coating

1 oz unsweetened baking chocolate

3 oz cacao butter

¼ tsp monk fruit powder

METHOD:

To Prepare the Filling;

Combine all ingredients in a medium mixing bowl, and mix to completely combine. Set the bowl in the fridge, and chill until firm, 30 minutes to one hour.

When the filling is set, scoop it into truffles using a tablespoon, and roll into round balls. Set the balls on a tray in the freezer to firm and chill them.

To Prepare the Chocolate Coating:

Combine all ingredients in the bowl of a double boiler.

Heat over medium until the ingredients are melted.

Remove the bowl from the heat, and stir to combine the ingredients, then set aside and allow the chocolate to cool slightly (this will help create a thicker layer on the truffles).

To Assemble:

Line a baking sheet with parchment paper, and set it aside.

Remove the truffle balls from the freezer.

One at a time, dip the balls into the chocolate coating, and roll them around to cover them completely. Place the dipped truffles on the prepared baking sheet. When they are all covered in chocolate, return them to the fridge to set the chocolate coating, about 30 minutes.

Store in an airtight container in the fridge up to two weeks.

DARK CHOCOLATE COVERED KEY LIME TRUFFLES

Prep: 15 mins

Cook/Chill: 1 hr 30 mins

Total: 1 hr 45 mins

Yield: 16-20 truffles

Nutrition for 2 from yield of 16: (includes chocolate coating)

Carbs	*Fat*	*Protein*
3g	*24g*	*2g*

INGREDIENTS:

Filling

¼ cup key lime juice

¼ cup coconut cream

½ cup coconut butter

½ cup almond flour

2 Tbsp coconut oil

1 tsp lime zest

½ tsp monk fruit powder

Chocolate Coating

1 oz unsweetened baking chocolate

3 oz cacao butter

¼ tsp monk fruit powder

METHOD:

To Prepare the Filling:

In a small saucepan, boil the key lime juice until it's reduced by half (there should be 2 tablespoons of juice left—this creates a stronger flavor for the truffle).

Combine all filling ingredients in the bowl of a food processor fitted with an "S" blade. Process until a smooth paste is formed.

Spoon the paste into silicone candy molds or into mini muffin tins lined with parchment paper liners.

Chill until the filling is set, one to two hours.

To Prepare the Chocolate Coating:

Combine all ingredients in the bowl of a double boiler.

Heat over medium until the ingredients are melted.

Remove the bowl from the heat, and stir to combine the ingredients. Set aside, and allow the chocolate to cool slightly (this will help create a thicker layer on the truffles).

To Assemble the Truffles:

Line a baking sheet with parchment paper, and set it aside.

When the truffle filling is set, remove it from the molds or muffin tins.

One at a time, dip the truffles in the prepared chocolate and roll around to coat. Repeat with all the truffles.

Place the prepared truffles on the baking sheet, and return them to the fridge to set the coating, about 30 minutes.

Store in an airtight container in the fridge for up to two weeks.

cookies

CHOCOLATE CHIP COOKIES

Prep: 45 mins

Cook: 15 mins

Total: 1 hour

Yield: 12-16 cookies

Nutrition for 2 from a yield of 12:

Carbs	*Fat*	*Protein*
2g	*16g*	*3g*

INGREDIENTS:

1½ cups almond flour

1 Tbsp erythritol

½ tsp monk fruit powder

¼ tsp salt

3 Tbsp full-fat coconut milk

¼ cup melted ghee or coconut oil

2 tsp vanilla

3 Tbsp cacao nibs OR ¼ cup sugar-free chocolate chips

METHOD:

Combine all ingredients except cacao nibs or chocolate chips in a medium mixing bowl, and mix to combine.

Add the cacao nibs or chocolate chips and mix to incorporate.

Transfer the dough to a piece of plastic wrap, and shape it into a log.

Place the dough in the freezer and chill until completely set, 20-30 minutes.

Preheat the oven to 350°F. Line a baking sheet with parchment paper.

When the dough is set, remove it from the freezer, unwrap it, and slice into ⅛-inch - ¼-inch rounds. Transfer them to the prepared baking sheet.

Bake the cookies 12-15 minutes, until they are mostly set.

Remove them from the oven and transfer them to a wire rack to cool completely.

Store in an airtight container on the counter up to two weeks.

***Note:** You can wrap the dough in a layer of foil and store it in the freezer up to two weeks.*

GRAHAM CRACKERS

Prep: 15 mins

Cook: 15 mins

Total: 30 mins

Yield: 8 cookies (equals 1 batch)

Nutrition for 2 from a yield of 8:

Carbs	Fat	Protein
2g	9g	2g

INGREDIENTS:

1 cup almond flour

2 Tbsp granulated erythritol

¼ tsp monk fruit extract

1 tsp ground flaxseed, optional (makes the cracker crispier)

½ tsp baking powder

⅛ tsp sea salt

3 Tbsp melted ghee or coconut oil

½ tsp vanilla extract

1 tsp molasses, optional (for more authentic "graham cracker" flavor)

METHOD:

Preheat the oven to 300°F.

Combine almond flour, erythritol, monk fruit extract, optional flaxseed, baking powder, and salt in a medium mixing bowl. Whisk to completely combine.

Add the coconut oil, vanilla, and optional molasses to the center of bowl, and stir them together as you mix to form a dough.

Roll out the dough between two pieces of parchment paper until it is about ⅛-inch–¼-inch thick, shaping the dough into a rectangle using your hands as you work.

Peel off the top piece of parchment paper, and transfer the bottom piece of parchment with the flattened dough rectangle onto a baking sheet.

Carefully cut the dough into eight to ten smaller rectangular crackers. Pierce each rectangle with a fork several times.

Bake for 15-20 minutes, until the crackers are golden and darkened around the edges.

When the crackers are done baking, remove them from the oven and cut the dough once again along the same lines.

Transfer the crackers to a wire rack to finish cooling.

Break apart, and enjoy! Store in an airtight container up to five days.

***Note:** To re-crisp the cookies, rebake them on a baking sheet in a 200°F oven for five minutes, and allow them to cool.*

CHOCOLATE WHOOPIE PIES

Prep: 15 mins

Cook: 45 mins

Total: 60 mins

Yield: 10-12 cookies

Nutrition for 2 from a yield of 12:

Carbs	Fat	Protein
4g	17g	5g

INGREDIENTS:

1 cup almond flour

¼ cup erythritol

1 tsp monk fruit powder

⅓ cup cacao powder

2 eggs

1 tsp vanilla

¼ cup melted ghee or coconut oil

¼ tsp salt

2 Tbsp full-fat coconut milk

½ cup vanilla buttercream (recipe page 51) or vanilla whipped cream frosting (recipe page 49)

METHOD:

Preheat the oven to 350°F. Line a baking sheet with parchment paper, and set aside.

Combine the almond flour, erythritol, monk fruit, and cacao powder in a medium bowl and mix to combine.

Add the eggs, vanilla, melted ghee or coconut oil, and salt. Mix to completely combine.

Add the coconut milk, and mix to form a smooth batter.

Scoop the batter by the tablespoon onto the prepared baking sheet, spreading the batter into an even 2-inch to 2½-inch circle and leaving about 1½ inches between each cookie.

Bake 8-12 minutes, until the cookies are set.

When the cookies are done baking, transfer them to a wire rack to cool completely before filling with the buttercream frosting.

Store in an airtight container in the fridge up to four days.

***Note:** To re-crisp the cookies, rebake them on a baking sheet in a 200°F oven for five minutes, and allow them to cool.*

COCONUT MACAROONS

Prep: 15 mins

Cook: 45 mins

Total: 60 mins

Yield: 10-12 cookies

Nutrition for 2 from a yield of 20:

Carbs	*Fat*	*Protein*
3g	*12g*	*2g*

INGREDIENTS:

1 cup coconut cream

1 Tbsp erythritol

¼ tsp monk fruit powder

1 tsp vanilla

1½ cups shredded coconut

½ cup almond flour

** If the coconut cream is solid, warm it in a saucepan until it's soft or slightly melted; this will allow you to mix it easily with the other ingredients.*

METHOD:

Preheat the oven to 350°. Line a baking sheet with parchment paper, and set it aside.

Combine all the ingredients in a medium mixing bowl, and mix well to completely combine.

Using a #40 scoop or a tablespoon measuring spoon, measure the coconut mixture into mounds on the prepared baking sheet.

Bake 15-20 minutes, until the edges just become slightly golden.

Allow the macaroons to cool completely before eating (or else they will fall apart!). You can transfer them to a cool baking sheet and into the freezer for 30 minutes to speed up this process.

Store in a sealed container in the fridge, or freezer up to one week. Enjoy!

WHITE CHOCOLATE MACADAMIA NUT COOKIES

Prep: 45 mins

Cook: 15 mins

Total: 1 hour

Yield: 12-16 cookies

Nutrition for 2 from a yield of 12:

Carbs	*Fat*	*Protein*
1g	*19g*	*2g*

INGREDIENTS:

1½ cups almond flour

1 Tbsp erythritol

½ tsp monk fruit powder

¼ tsp salt

3 Tbsp full-fat coconut milk

¼ cup melted cacao butter

2 tsp vanilla

⅓ cup chopped toasted macadamia nuts (to mix in)

METHOD:

Combine all ingredients except macadamia nuts in a medium mixing bowl, and mix to combine.

Add the macadamia nuts and mix to incorporate.

Transfer the dough to a piece of plastic wrap, and shape it into a log.

Place the dough in the freezer and chill until completely set, 20-30 minutes.

Preheat the oven to 350°F. Line a baking sheet with parchment paper.

When the dough is set, remove it from the freezer, unwrap it, and slice into ⅛-inch–¼-inch rounds. Transfer them to the prepared baking sheet.

Bake the cookies 12-15 minutes, until they are mostly set.

Remove them from the oven and transfer them to a wire rack to cool completely.

Store in an airtight container on the counter up to 1 week.

***Note:** You can wrap the dough in a layer of foil and store it in the fridge up to two weeks.*

SLICE 'N BAKE SUGAR COOKIES

Prep: 45 mins

Cook: 15 mins

Total: 1 hour

Yield: 12-16 cookies

Nutrition for 2 from a yield of 12:

Carbs	Fat	Protein
2g	10g	2g

INGREDIENTS:

1½ cups almond flour

1 Tbsp erythritol

½ tsp monk fruit powder

¼ tsp salt

3 Tbsp full-fat coconut milk

¼ cup melted ghee or coconut oil

2 tsp vanilla

METHOD:

Combine all ingredients in a medium mixing bowl, and mix to combine.

Transfer the dough to a piece of plastic wrap, and shape it into a log.

Place the dough in the freezer, and chill until completely set, 20-30 minutes.

Preheat the oven to 350°F. Line a baking sheet with parchment paper.

When the dough is set, remove it from the freezer, unwrap it, and slice into ⅛-inch–¼-inch rounds. Transfer them to the prepared baking sheet.

Bake the cookies 12-15 minutes, until they are mostly set.

Remove them from the oven and transfer them to a wire rack to cool completely.

Store in an airtight container on the counter up to 1 week.

Note: You can wrap the dough in a layer of foil and store it in the fridge up to two weeks.

OREOS

Prep: 45 mins

Cook/Chill: 45 mins

Total: 1 hr 30 mins

Yield: 10-12 cookies

Nutrition for 2 from a yield of 10:

Carbs	*Fat*	*Protein*
3g	*26g*	*5g*

INGREDIENTS:

1½ cups almond flour

⅓ cup cacao powder

1 tsp baking powder

¼ cup erythritol

1 tsp monk fruit powder

¼ tsp salt

1 tsp vanilla

1 egg

2 Tbsp melted coconut oil

1 cup vanilla buttercream frosting (recipe page 55)

METHOD:

Combine all ingredients in a medium mixing bowl, and mix to combine.

Transfer the dough to a piece of plastic wrap, and shape it into a log.

Place the dough in the freezer, and chill until completely set, 20-30 minutes.

Preheat the oven to 350°F. Line a baking sheet with parchment paper.

When the dough is set, remove it from the freezer, unwrap it, and slice thinly into ⅛-inch–¼-inch rounds. Transfer them to the prepared baking sheet (try to slice an even number of cookies so you can turn them all into delicious Oreos!).

Bake the cookies 10-12 minutes, until they are mostly set.

Remove them from the oven, and transfer them to a wire rack to cool completely.

To prepare the cookie sandwiches, spoon 2 teaspoons of frosting onto one cookie, and top the frosting with a second cookie. Repeat until all cookies have been filled and paired. Chill the cookies 30 minutes to set the filling.

Store in an airtight container in the fridge up to 1 week.

Note: You can wrap the dough in a layer of foil, and store it in the fridge up to two weeks.

LEMON BARS

Prep: 30 mins

Cook/Chill: 1 hr 30 mins

Total: 2 hours

Yield: 16 bars

Nutrition for 2 from a yield of 16:

Carbs	Fat	Protein
2g	16g	2g

INGREDIENTS:

*½ of an unbaked flaky keto pie crust**

½ cup lemon juice

½ cup melted coconut oil

¼ cup erythritol

Zest of 2 lemons

3 large eggs

1 Tbsp gelatin

1 tsp monk fruit powder

Note: see pie chapter

METHOD:

Preheat the oven to 350°F. Line an 8-inch x 8-inch baking dish with parchment paper.

Partially roll out the pie dough, then press it into an even layer in the prepared baking dish.

Bake the crust 10-15 minutes until it's set. Remove it from the oven and allow it to cool fully before filling.

In a small saucepan, heat the lemon juice, coconut oil, erythritol, and lemon zest until warm.

While the lemon mixture is warming, whisk the eggs in a medium mixing bowl. Slowly pour the warm lemon juice mixture into the eggs in a thin stream, whisking constantly to temper the eggs.

Whisk in the gelatin.

Return the mixture to the saucepan and whisk in the monk fruit. Return the pan to the stove over medium-low to heat through, stirring constantly.

When the filling begins to thicken, pour it into prepared cooled pie crust.

Bake 20-25 minutes, until the center is set but still jiggles a little bit.

Remove the lemon bars from the oven, and cool completely before refrigerating to set (one hour or overnight).

To serve, remove the bars from the baking dish and slice into 16 squares.

Store in an airtight container in the fridge up to three days.

CINNAMON ALMOND BUTTER COOKIES

Prep: 15 mins

Cook: 10 mins

Total: 25 mins

Yield: 25 cookies

Nutrition for 2 from a yield of 16:

Carbs	Fat	Protein
2g	18g	9g

INGREDIENTS:

1 cup creamy almond butter

½ cup almond flour

¼ cup granulated erythritol

¾ tsp monk fruit powder

1 Tbsp cinnamon

½ tsp salt

1 tsp vanilla

2 eggs

METHOD:

Preheat the oven to 350°F. Line a baking sheet with parchment paper, and set aside.

In a medium bowl, combine the almond butter, almond flour, erythritol, monk fruit powder, cinnamon, salt, and vanilla. Mix to completely combine.

Add the eggs, and mix to form a smoother dough.

Scoop the dough by the heaping tablespoon, and roll it into balls. Flatten the balls with your hands, and place them on the prepared baking sheet.

Bake the cookies for 10-12 minutes, until edges are cooked and the cookies are set.

Remove the cookies and transfer them to a wire rack to cool fully before serving.

Store in an airtight container on the counter up to five days.

PECAN SANDIES

Prep: 45 mins

Cook: 15 mins

Total: 1 hour

Yield: 12-16 cookies

Nutrition for 2 from a yield of 12:

Carbs	*Fat*	*Protein*
1g	22g	2g

INGREDIENTS:

*¾ cup pecan flour**

¾ cup almond flour

½ tsp sea salt

1 Tbsp erythritol

½ tsp monk fruit powder

3 Tbsp coconut milk

1 tsp vanilla

¼ cup melted coconut oil

⅓ cup chopped toasted pecans (to mix in)

METHOD:

Combine all ingredients except chopped pecan in a medium mixing bowl. Mix to combine.

Add the chopped pecans, and mix to incorporate.

Transfer the dough to a piece of plastic wrap, and shape it into a log.

Place the dough in the freezer, and chill until completely set, 20-30 minutes.

Preheat the oven to 350°F. Line a baking sheet with parchment paper.

When the dough is set, remove it from the freezer, unwrap it, and slice into ⅛-inch–¼-inch rounds. Transfer them to the prepared baking sheet.

Bake the cookies 12-15 minutes, until they are mostly set.

Remove them from the oven, and transfer them to a wire rack to cool completely.

Store in an airtight container on the counter up to seven days.

** To make pecan flour, transfer 1 cup of pecans to a food processor fitted with an "S" blade, and process until they are mostly powdered.*

Note: You can wrap the dough in a layer of foil, and store it in the fridge up to two weeks.

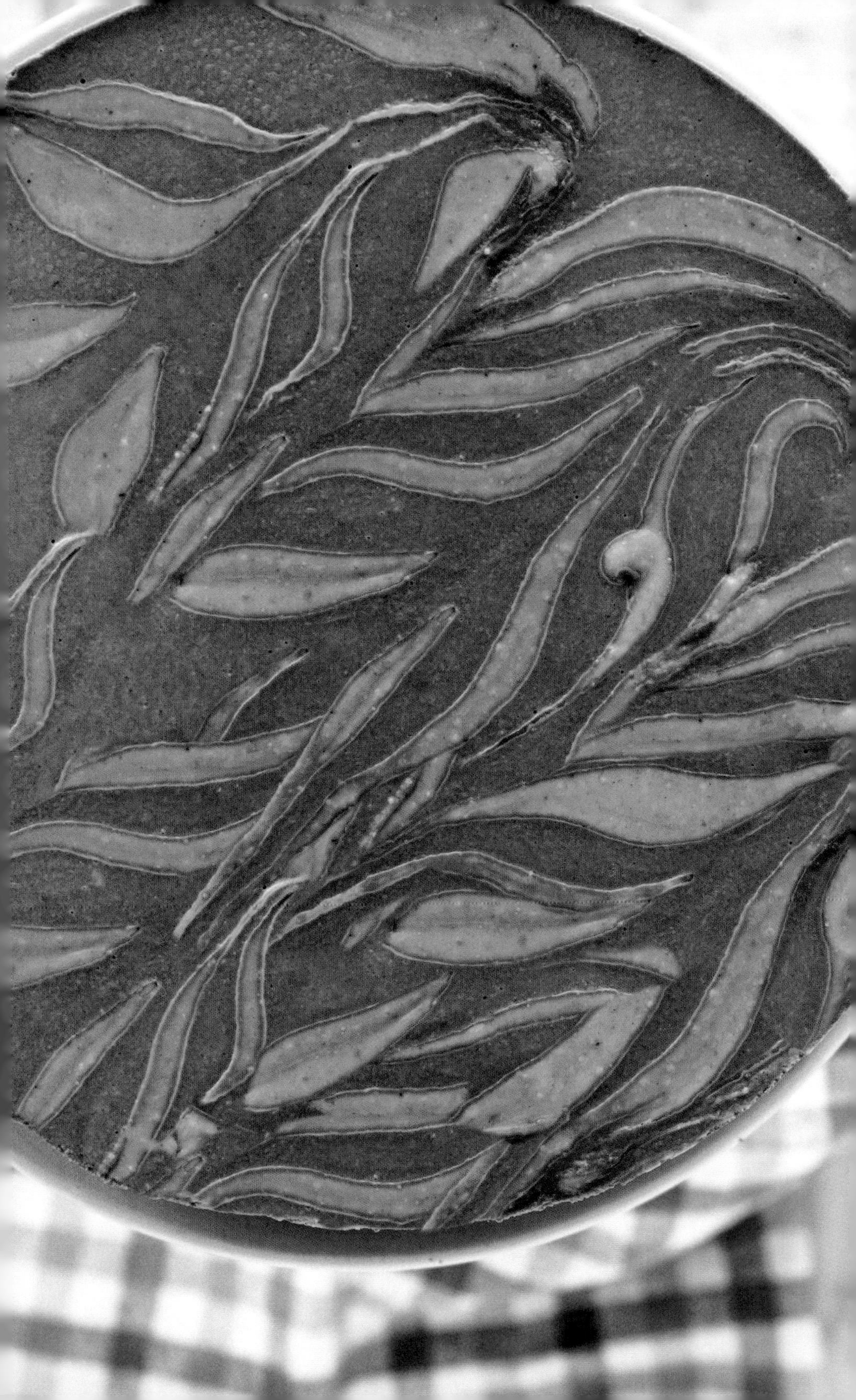

cheesecake

Graham Cracker Crust for Cheesecake

Chocolate Graham Cracker Crust for Cheesecake

Vanilla Cheesecake

Lemon Cheesecake

Key Lime Cheesecake

Chocolate Cheesecake

White Chocolate Raspberry Cheesecake

White Chocolate Peppermint Cheesecake

Layered Mocha Cheesecake

Chocolate Hazelnut Butter Swirl Cheesecake

GRAHAM CRACKER CRUST FOR CHEESECAKE

Prep: 10 mins

Cook: 10 mins

Total: 20 mins

Yield: 1 crust

Nutrition for 1 slice of 16:

Carbs	Fat	Protein
1g	6g	2g

INGREDIENTS:

1 batch of Graham Crackers (recipe page 109)

1 egg white

METHOD:

Preheat the oven to 350°F. Line the bottom of a springform pan with parchment paper, and set it aside.

Break the graham crackers into pieces, and transfer them to the bowl of a food processor fitted with an "S" blade. Process them into a powder.

Add the egg white, and process until a dough forms.

Press the dough into the bottom of the prepared springform pan. Bake for 10 minutes or until set.

Allow the crust to cool completely before adding the filling.

CHOCOLATE GRAHAM CRACKER CRUST FOR CHEESECAKE

Prep: 10 mins

Cook: 10 mins

Total: 20 mins

Yield: 1 crust

Nutrition for 1 slice of 16:

Carbs	Fat	Protein
3g	6g	2g

INGREDIENTS:

1 batch of Graham Crackers (recipe page 109)

3 Tbsp cacao powder

1 egg white

METHOD:

Preheat the oven to 350°F. Line the bottom of a springform pan with parchment paper, and set it aside.

Break the graham crackers into pieces, and transfer them to the bowl of a food processor fitted with an "S" blade. Add the cacao powder, and process everything into a powder.

Add the egg white, and process until a dough forms.

Press the dough into the bottom of the prepared springform pan. Bake for 10 minutes or until set.

Allow the crust to cool completely before adding the filling.

VANILLA CHEESECAKE

Prep: 10 mins

Chill: 2 hours

Total: 2 hrs 10 mins

Yield: 12-16 slices

Nutrition for 1 slice of 16:

Carbs	Fat	Protein
4g	22g	4g

INGREDIENTS:

1 Graham Cracker Crust for Cheesecake (recipe page 128)

1½ cups raw macadamia nuts, soaked overnight

2 cups coconut cream

¼ cup water

1 Tbsp gelatin + 1 tsp

¼ cup boiling water

1 tsp monk fruit powder

½ cup granulated erythritol

¼ cup lemon juice

1 tsp apple cider vinegar

2 tsp vanilla extract

¼ tsp vanilla powder

⅛ tsp salt

METHOD:

Drain the macadamia nuts, and discard the soak water.

Combine all ingredients (except the crust) in a high-powered blender, and blend until smooth.

Pour the mixture into the prepared 7-inch crust, and chill two hours or until set.

Store covered in the fridge for up to four days.

LEMON CHEESECAKE

Prep: 10 mins

Chill: 2 hours

Total: 2 hrs 10 mins

Yield: 12-16 slices

Nutrition for 1 slice of 16:

Carbs	Fat	Protein
4g	22g	4g

INGREDIENTS:

1 Graham Cracker Crust for Cheesecake (recipe page 128)

1½ cups raw macadamia nuts, soaked overnight

2 cups coconut cream

1 Tbsp gelatin + 1 tsp

¼ cup boiling water

1 tsp monk fruit powder

½ cup granulated erythritol

½ cup key lime juice

1 tsp apple cider vinegar

2 tsp vanilla extract

¼ tsp vanilla powder

⅛ tsp salt

METHOD:

Drain the macadamia nuts, and discard the soak water.

Combine all ingredients (except the crust) in a high-powered blender and blend until smooth.

Pour the mixture into the prepared 7-inch crust, and chill two hours or until set.

Store covered in the fridge for up to four days.

KEY LIME CHEESECAKE

Prep: 10 mins

Chill: 2 hours

Total: 2 hrs 10 mins

Yield: 12-16 slices

Nutrition for 1 slice of 16:

Carbs	*Fat*	*Protein*
4g	*22g*	*4g*

INGREDIENTS:

1 Graham Cracker Crust for Cheesecake (recipe page 128)

1½ cups raw macadamia nuts, soaked overnight

2 cups coconut cream

1 Tbsp gelatin + 1 tsp

¼ cup boiling water

1 tsp monk fruit powder

½ cup granulated erythritol

½ cup key lime juice

1 tsp apple cider vinegar

2 tsp vanilla extract

¼ tsp vanilla powder

⅛ tsp salt

METHOD:

Drain the macadamia nuts, and discard the soak water.

Combine all ingredients (except the crust) in a high-powered blender, and blend until smooth.

Pour the mixture into the prepared 7-inch crust, and chill two hours or until set.

Store covered in the fridge for up to four days.

CHOCOLATE CHEESECAKE

Prep: 10 mins

Chill: 2 hours

Total: 2 hrs 10 mins

Yield: 12-16 slices

Nutrition for 1 slice of 16:

Carbs	Fat	Protein
5g	22g	4g

INGREDIENTS:

1 Graham Cracker Crust for Cheesecake (recipe page 128)

1½ cups raw macadamia nuts, soaked overnight

2 cups coconut cream

¼ cup water

1 Tbsp gelatin

¼ cup boiling water

1 tsp monk fruit powder

½ cup granulated erythritol

¼ cup lemon juice

1 tsp apple cider vinegar

1 tsp vanilla extract

⅔ cup cacao powder

⅛ tsp salt

METHOD:

Drain the macadamia nuts, and discard the soak water.

Combine all ingredients (except the crust) in a high-powered blender, and blend until smooth.

Pour the mixture into the prepared 7-inch crust, and chill two hours or until set.

Store covered in the fridge for up to four days.

WHITE CHOCOLATE RASPBERRY CHEESECAKE

Prep: 10 mins

Chillk: 2 hours

Total: 2 hrs 10 mins

Yield: 12-16 slices

Nutrition for 1 slice of 16:

Carbs	*Fat*	*Protein*
4g	*25g*	*4g*

INGREDIENTS:

1 Graham Cracker Crust for Cheesecake (recipe page 128)

1½ cups raw macadamia nuts, soaked overnight

1½ cups coconut cream

6 Tbsp melted cacao butter

¼ cup water

1 Tbsp gelatin

¼ cup boiling water

1 tsp monk fruit powder

½ cup granulated erythritol

¼ cup lemon juice

1 tsp apple cider vinegar

2 tsp vanilla extract

¼ tsp vanilla powder

⅛ tsp salt

6 oz raspberries, fresh or frozen (to sprinkle on top)

METHOD:

Drain the macadamia nuts, and discard the soak water.

Combine all ingredients (except the crust) in a high-powered blender, and blend until smooth.

Pour the mixture into the prepared 7-inch crust, and sprinkle the raspberries over the top, pressing them down slightly into the filling.

Chill two hours or until set.

Store covered in the fridge for up to four days.

WHITE CHOCOLATE PEPPERMINT CHEESECAKE

Prep: 10 mins

Chill: 4 hours

Total: 4 hrs 10 mins

Yield: 12-16 slices

Nutrition for 1 slice of 16:

Carbs	Fat	Protein
3g	25g	3g

INGREDIENTS:

1 Graham Cracker Crust for Cheesecake (recipe page 128)

1½ cups raw macadamia nuts, soaked overnight

1½ cups coconut cream

6 Tbsp melted cacao butter

¼ cup water

1 Tbsp gelatin

¼ cup boiling water

1 tsp monk fruit powder

½ cup granulated erythritol

¼ cup lemon juice

1 tsp apple cider vinegar

1 tsp vanilla extract

1 Tbsp peppermint extract

¼ tsp vanilla powder

⅛ tsp salt

30 drops liquid chlorophyll, optional (for color)

METHOD:

Drain the macadamia nuts, and discard the soak water.

Combine all ingredients (except the chlorophyll and crust) in a high-powered blender, and blend until smooth. Pour off ¾ cup of the filling. Combine it with the optional chlorophyll, and set it aside.

Pour the remaining filling to the prepared crust.

Drizzle the ¾ cup of green filling in a back-and-forth motion over the rest of the batter. Run a knife back and forth across the batter to create the swirl pattern.

Chill four hours or overnight, until set.

Store covered in the fridge for up to four days.

LAYERED MOCHA CHEESECAKE

Prep: 10 mins

Chill: 2 hours

Total: 2 hrs 10 mins

Yield: 12-16 slices

Nutrition for 1 slice of 16:

Carbs	*Fat*	*Protein*
4g	*22g*	*4g*

INGREDIENTS:

1 Graham Cracker Crust for Cheesecake (recipe page 128)

1½ cups raw macadamia nuts, soaked overnight

2 cups coconut cream

¼ cup water

1 Tbsp gelatin + 1 tsp

¼ cup boiling water

1 tsp monk fruit powder

½ cup granulated erythritol

¼ cup lemon juice

1 tsp apple cider vinegar

2 tsp vanilla extract

¼ tsp vanilla powder

⅛ tsp salt

1½ tsp ground espresso

¼ cup cacao powder

METHOD:

Drain the macadamia nuts, and discard the soak water.

Combine all the ingredients (except the crust, the ground espresso, and the cacao powder) in a high-powered blender, and blend until smooth.

Pour half the batter into a small bowl, and stir in the ground espresso. Pour this half of the batter into the prepared springform pan, and freeze it to set, about 30 minutes.

Add the cacao powder to the remaining half of the batter, and blend to combine it.

When the espresso layer is set, pour the chocolate layer over it, and transfer the entire cheesecake to the fridge to set completely, two hours or overnight.

Store covered in the fridge for up to four days.

CHOCOLATE HAZELNUT BUTTER SWIRL CHEESECAKE

Prep: 10 mins

Chill: 4 hours

Total: 4 hrs 10 mins

Yield: 12-16 slices

Nutrition for 1 slice of 16:

Carbs	Fat	Protein
5g	22g	7g

INGREDIENTS:

1 Graham Cracker Crust for Cheesecake (recipe page 128)

1½ cups raw macadamia nuts, soaked overnight

2 cups coconut cream

¼ cup water

1 Tbsp gelatin + 1 tsp

¼ cup boiling water

1 tsp monk fruit powder

½ cup granulated erythritol

¼ cup lemon juice

1 tsp apple cider vinegar

2 tsp vanilla extract

¼ tsp vanilla powder

⅛ tsp salt

⅔ cup cacao powder

⅔ cup hazelnut butter, divided (to swirl)

METHOD:

Drain the macadamia nuts, and discard the soak water.

Combine all the ingredients (except the crust and the hazelnut butter) in a high-powered blender, and blend until smooth.

Pour ⅓ cup hazelnut butter into the prepared crust, and spread it into an even layer. Freeze for 15 minutes to set.

When the hazelnut butter is somewhat set, pour the cheesecake batter over it.

Drizzle the remaining hazelnut butter in a back-and-forth motion over the cheesecake. Then drag a butter knife back and forth across the batter to create the swirl pattern.

Place the cheesecake in the fridge, and chill four hours or until set.

Store covered in the fridge for up to four days.

popsicles

Blueberry Cardamom Popsicles

Chocolate Raspberry Popsicles

Toasted Coconut Popsicles

Cucumber Lime Mint Ice Pops

Key Lime “Pie-cicles”

Strawberries & Cream Popsicles

Lemonade Ice Pops

BLUEBERRY CARDAMOM POPSICLES

Prep: 5 mins

Chill: 4 hours

Total: 4 hrs 5 mins

Yield: 6 x 3 oz popsicles

Nutrition for 1 popsicle:

Carbs	Fat	Protein
8g	12g	0g

INGREDIENTS:

1 can full-fat coconut milk (can size 13.5 - 15 oz)

2 cups fresh blueberries

½ tsp monk fruit powder

½ tsp ground cardamom

METHOD:

Combine all ingredients in the blender, and blend until smooth.

Pour the mixture into your popsicle molds, and freeze until completely set, four hours or overnight.

Store in the freezer up to two weeks.

CHOCOLATE RASPBERRY POPSICLES

Prep: 5 mins

Chill: 4 hours

Total: 4 hrs 5 mins

Yield: 6 x 3 oz popsicles

Nutrition for 1 popsicle:

Carbs	Fat	Protein
6g	8g	2g

INGREDIENTS:

2 Tbsp erythritol

1 tsp monk fruit powder

1 can full-fat coconut milk (can size 13.5 - 15 oz)

1 pints raspberries

¼ cup cacao powder

1 Tbsp gelatin

METHOD:

Combine all ingredients in the blender, and blend until smooth.

Pour the mixture into your popsicle molds, and freeze until completely set, four hours or overnight.

Store in the freezer up to two weeks.

TOASTED COCONUT POPSICLES

Prep: 5 mins

Chill: 4 hours

Total: 4 hrs 5 mins

Yield: 6 x 3 oz popsicles

Nutrition for 1 popsicle:

Carbs	Fat	Protein
3g	25g	1g

INGREDIENTS:

½ cup coconut butter

1 can of coconut milk

2 Tbsp erythritol

1 tsp monk fruit powder

1 Tbsp gelatin

METHOD:

Heat coconut butter over medium until it becomes golden (watch carefully, it goes from golden to brown very quickly!).

Combine all ingredients in the blender, and blend until smooth.

Pour the mixture into your popsicle molds, and freeze until completely set, four hours or overnight.

Store in the freezer up to two weeks.

CUCUMBER LIME MINT ICE POPS

Prep: 5 mins

Chill: 4 hours

Total: 4 hrs 5 mins

Yield: 6 x 3 oz popsicles

Nutrition for 1 popsicle:

Carbs	Fat	Protein
2g	0g	0g

INGREDIENTS:

1½ cups chopped cucumber

1 cup water

3 Tbsp lime juice

15-20 mint leaves

2 Tbsp erythritol

1 tsp monk fruit powder

Dash of sea salt

METHOD:

Combine all ingredients in the blender, and blend until smooth.

Pour the mixture into your popsicle molds, and freeze until completely set, four hours or overnight.

Store in the freezer up to two weeks.

KEY LIME "PIE-CICLES"

Prep: 5 mins

Chill: 4 hours

Total: 4 hrs 5 mins

Yield: 6 x 3 oz popsicles

Nutrition for 1 popsicle:

Carbs	Fat	Protein
4g	7g	1g

INGREDIENTS:

⅓ cup key lime juice

1 can full-fat coconut milk (can size 13.5 - 15 oz)

1 tsp fresh lime zest

2 Tbsp erythritol

1 tsp monk fruit powder

1 Tbsp gelatin

METHOD:

Combine all ingredients in the blender, and blend until smooth.

Pour the mixture into your popsicle molds, and freeze until completely set, four hours or overnight.

Store in the freezer up to two weeks.

STRAWBERRIES & CREAM POPSICLES

Prep: 5 mins

Chill: 4 hours

Total: 4 hrs 5 mins

Yield: 6 x 3 oz popsicles

Nutrition for 1 popsicle:

Carbs	Fat	Protein
3g	13g	1g

INGREDIENTS:

1 can full-fat coconut milk (can size 13.5 - 15 oz)

1 cup chopped strawberries

1 Tbsp lemon juice

2 Tbsp erythritol

1 tsp monk fruit powder

1 Tbsp gelatin

METHOD:

Combine all ingredients in the blender, and blend until smooth.

Pour the mixture into your popsicle molds, and freeze until completely set, four hours or overnight.

Store in the freezer up to two weeks.

LEMONADE ICE POPS

Prep: 5 mins

Chill: 4 hours

Total: 4 hrs 5 mins

Yield: 6 x 3 oz popsicles

Nutrition for 1 popsicle:

Carbs	Fat	Protein
2g	0g	0g

INGREDIENTS:

¾ cup lemon juice

1½ cups water

2 Tbsp erythritol

1 tsp monk fruit powder

METHOD:

Combine all ingredients in the blender, and blend until smooth.

Pour the mixture into your popsicle molds, and freeze until completely set, four hours or overnight.

Store in the freezer up to two weeks.

***Note:** If you can't wait for the pops to freeze, pour the mixture over ice, and drink it as lemonade!*

pies

Flaky Keto Pie Crust
Graham Cracker Pie Crust for Pie
Coconut Pie Crust
Custard Pie
Lemon Meringue Pie
French Coconut Pie
Chocolate Mousse Pie
Key Lime Pie

FLAKY KETO PIE CRUST

Prep: 40 mins

Cook: 30 mins

Total: 1 hrs 10 mins

Yield: 1 crust

Nutrition for 1 slice of 16:

Carbs	Fat	Protein
1g	10g	2g

INGREDIENTS:

1 cup almond flour

½ cup coconut flour

½ tsp sea salt

½ cup palm shortening

¼ cup water

METHOD:

Preheat the oven to 350°F.

Combine the almond flour, coconut flour, and salt in a medium bowl, and mix to combine.

Add the palm shortening, and use a form to mix and press the flour and shortening together, creating a crumbly dough.

Add the water, and mix to combine and form a smooth dough.

Wrap the dough in plastic wrap and refrigerate 30 minutes or overnight. Remove the dough from the fridge, and allow it to sit out five minutes.

When the dough is ready, unwrap the dough and place it between two pieces of parchment paper. Press the dough down slightly, and then use a rolling pin to roll the dough into a ¼-inch thick, 12-inch to 15-inch wide circle. When the dough is formed, remove the top sheet of parchment paper, and smooth the edges to even them out.

Place a 9-inch pie pan upside down on top of the dough. Carefully turn the dough and pie pan right-side up, so the dough is resting in the pie pan and the sheet of parchment paper is on top. Carefully press the dough into the pie pan, and gently remove the parchment paper.

Use your fingers to even out the edges and smooth the cracks until the pie crust is formed in the pan. Use a fork to poke holes in the bottom of the crust for even baking.

Bake the crust 20 minutes, until firm to the touch and very lightly golden on the edges.

Allow the pie crust to cool completely before filling.

GRAHAM CRACKER CRUST FOR PIE

Prep: 5 mins

Cook: 10 mins

Total: 15 mins

Yield: 1 crust

Nutrition for 1 slice of 16:

Carbs	Fat	Protein
3g	0g	0g

INGREDIENTS:

1 batch of Graham Crackers (recipe page 109)

1 egg white

METHOD:

Preheat the oven to 350°F.

Break the graham crackers into pieces, and transfer them to the bowl of a food processor fitted with an "S" blade. Process them into a powder.

Add the egg white, and process until a dough forms.

Press the dough into an 8-inch pie pan, and use your hands to press it evenly up the sides and over the bottom.

Bake for 10 minutes or until set.

Allow the crust to cool completely before adding the filling.

COCONUT PIE CRUST

Prep: 40 mins

Cook: 10 mins

Total: 50 mins

Yield: 1 crust

Nutrition for 1 slice of 16:

Carbs	Fat	Protein
1g	6g	1g

INGREDIENTS:

1 egg white

¼ tsp monk fruit powder

Dash of sea salt

2 tsp coconut oil

1½ cups shredded coconut

METHOD:

Preheat the oven to 325°F.

Whip the egg white with the monk fruit and salt, until the mixture is foamy but not stiff.

Add the shredded coconut, and mix to thoroughly combine the egg white with the coconut.

Use the coconut oil to grease a 9-inch pie tin.

Press the shredded coconut mixture into the pie tin and up the sides, in an even layer.

Bake the crust 10-12 minutes, until the edges are golden brown. Allow the crust to cool completely before using*.

** If you're using this pie crust for another pie that is baked (for example, the key lime pie), cover the edges of the crust with foil before the second baking so the crust doesn't burn.*

CUSTARD PIE

Prep: 10 mins

Cook: 45 mins

Total: 55 mins

Yield: 12-16 slices

Nutrition for 1 slice of 16:

Carbs	Fat	Protein
5g	19g	2g

INGREDIENTS:

Crust:

One 8-inch to 9-inch flaky keto pie crust, pre-baked for 10 minutes (recipe page 165)

Filling:

4 eggs

2½ cups full-fat coconut milk

½ tsp monk fruit powder

¼ cup erythritol

1 tsp vanilla

¼ tsp salt

2 tsp gelatin

¼ tsp nutmeg (to sprinkle)

METHOD:

Preheat the oven to 400°F.

Separate one egg and set the white aside. Combine remaining ingredients, and mix well until combined.

Whip the first egg white until stiff peaks form. Add the egg white to the milk mixture, and whisk until just incorporated.

Pour the filling into the pie shell, and bake 45-50 minutes until the top is browned. Remove the pie, and sprinkle the nutmeg over it.

Allow it to cool completely before slicing and serving.

LEMON MERINGUE PIE

Prep: 20 mins

Cook/Chill: 2 hrs 20 mins

Total: 2 hrs 40 mins

Yield: 12-16 slices

Nutrition for 1 slice of 16:

Carbs	*Fat*	*Protein*
2g	*11g*	*3g*

INGREDIENTS:

Crust:

One 8-inch to 9-inch flaky keto pie crust, pre-baked for 10 minutes (recipe page 165)

Filling:

1 Tbsp + ½ tsp gelatin

1 cup water, divided

½ cup lemon juice

½ cup granulated erythritol

1 whole egg

4 egg yolks

3 Tbsp arrowroot starch

1 tsp monk fruit powder

2 tsp lemon zest

3 Tbsp melted coconut oil or ghee

Meringue:

4 egg whites

Dash of salt

⅓ cup granulated erythritol

¼ tsp monk fruit powder

1 tsp vanilla

METHOD:

To Prepare the Filling:

In a small bowl, combine the gelatin and ½ cup water, and whisk to combine. Set aside.

In a medium saucepan, heat the lemon juice, erythritol, and remaining ½ cup water to dissolve the erythritol.

While the juice is warming, combine the eggs and the egg yolk with the arrowroot starch, monk fruit powder, and lemon zest in a medium mixing bowl and whisk to combine.

When the lemon juice mixture is warm, slowly pour it over the egg mixture in a thin stream, whisking constantly to temper the eggs.

Return the mixture to the saucepan, add the coconut oil and gelatin mixture, and heat it over medium-low until it begins to thicken, stirring constantly. When the mixture begins to thicken, remove it from the heat and set it aside.

To Prepare the Meringue:

Preheat the oven to 350°F.

In a clean bowl, whip the egg whites with dash of salt, erythritol, monk fruit, and vanilla until they are shiny and form stiff peaks.

Pour the pie filling into the prepared pie crust.

Use a large spoon to dollop the meringue over the hot pie filling.

Bake the pie for 20 minutes, until the top of the meringue is lightly golden and filling is mostly set.

Chill completely in the fridge for two hours before slicing.

Store covered in the fridge for up to four days.

FRENCH COCONUT PIE

Prep: 5 mins

Cook: 40 mins

Total: 45 mins

Yield: 12-16 slices

Nutrition for 1 slice of 16:

Carbs	Fat	Protein
3g	20g	1g

INGREDIENTS:

Crust:

One 8-inch to 9-inch flaky keto pie crust, pre-baked for 10 minutes (recipe page 165)

Filling:

¼ cup erythritol

1 tsp monk fruit powder

3 eggs

1 Tbsp apple cider vinegar

1 14.5 oz can coconut milk

⅓ cup coconut oil, melted

1 tsp vanilla

1½ cups shredded coconut

METHOD:

Preheat the oven to 350°F.

Combine all ingredients in a large mixing bowl. Mix to completely combine.

Bake the pie 40-45 minutes, until the center is set.

Allow the pie to cool completely before slicing and serving.

Store covered in the fridge for up to four days.

CHOCOLATE MOUSSE PIE

Prep: 5 mins

Chill: 2 hours

Total: 2 hrs 5 mins

Yield: 12-16 slices

Nutrition for 1 slice of 16:

Carbs	Fat	Protein
3g	14g	2g

INGREDIENTS:

Crust:

One 8-inch to 9-inch flaky keto pie crust, pre-baked for 10 minutes (recipe page 165)

Filling:

2 cups coconut cream

½ cup water

1 Tbsp gelatin

½ cup boiling water

2 tsp vanilla

⅓ cup cacao powder

3 Tbsp erythritol

1¼ tsp monk fruit powder

¼ tsp salt

METHOD:

Combine all ingredients in a high-powered blender, and blend until completely smooth.

Pour the filling into the prepared pie crust.

Chill in the fridge until set, about two hours or overnight.

Top with vanilla whipped cream and dark chocolate shavings, if desired.

Store covered in the fridge up to four days.

KEY LIME PIE

Prep: 5 mins

Cook: 20 mins

Total: 25 mins

Yield: 12-16 slices

Nutrition for 1 slice of 16:

Carbs	Fat	Protein
3g	11g	2g

INGREDIENTS:

Crust:

One 8-inch to 9-inch flaky keto pie crust, pre-baked for 10 minutes (recipe page 165)

Filling:

½ cup coconut cream

½ cup coconut milk

2 Tbsp erythritol

1½ tsp monk fruit powder

½ cup key lime juice

3 large eggs

2 Tbsp arrowroot starch

1 tsp gelatin

METHOD:

Preheat the oven to 350°F.

Combine all filling ingredients in a high-powered blender, and blend until completely combined.

Pour the filling into the prepared pie crust.

Bake 20-25 minutes until the center is set but still jiggles a little bit.

Cool completely before refrigerating to set, then top with whipped vanilla frosting and serve.

Store covered in the fridge up to four days.

Panna Cotta & Crème Brûlée

VANILLA PANNA COTTA

Prep: 10 mins

Cook/Chill: 4 hrs 10 mins

Total: 4 hrs 20 mins

Yield: 4 x 4 oz custards

Nutrition for 1 custard:

Carbs	Fat	Protein
5g	24g	0g

INGREDIENTS:

2½ tsp gelatin

2 cups full-fat coconut milk

½ tsp monk fruit powder

1 tsp vanilla

METHOD:

Combine gelatin and coconut milk in a small saucepan, and whisk to combine. Set aside to let the gelatin soak for five minutes.

When the gelatin has soaked, add the monk fruit and vanilla, and whisk to combine completely.

Warm the mixture over medium heat to melt gelatin.

When the mixture is warmed, evenly distribute it between four 4-ounce ramekins, and chill four hours or overnight.

Store covered in the fridge up to five days.

CHOCOLATE PANNA COTTA

Prep: 10 mins

Cook/Chill: 4 hrs 10 mins

Total: 4 hrs 20 mins

Yield: 4 x 4 oz custards

Nutrition for 1 custard:

Carbs	Fat	Protein
4g	23g	3g

INGREDIENTS:

2 tsp gelatin

2 cups full-fat coconut milk

½ tsp monk fruit powder

1 tsp vanilla

3 Tbsp cacao powder

1 Tbsp erythritol

METHOD:

Combine gelatin and coconut milk in a small saucepan, and whisk to combine. Set aside to let the gelatin soak for five minutes.

When the gelatin has soaked, add the monk fruit, vanilla, cacao powder, and erythritol, and whisk to combine completely.

Warm the mixture over medium heat to melt gelatin.

When the mixture is warmed, evenly distribute it between four 4-ounce ramekins and chill four hours or overnight.

Store covered in the fridge up to five days.

RASBERRY PANNA COTTA

Prep: 10 mins

Cook/Chill: 4 hrs 10 mins

Total: 4 hrs 20 mins

Yield: 4 x 4 oz custards

Nutrition for 1 custard:

Carbs	Fat	Protein
7g	23g	3g

INGREDIENTS:

2½ tsp gelatin

2 cups full-fat coconut milk

½ tsp monk fruit powder

1 tsp vanilla

6 oz fresh raspberries

1 Tbsp lemon juice

METHOD:

Combine gelatin and coconut milk in a small saucepan and whisk to combine. Set aside to let the gelatin soak for five minutes.

When the gelatin has soaked, add the monk fruit and vanilla, and whisk to combine completely.

Warm the mixture over medium heat to melt gelatin.

When the mixture is warmed, transfer it to a high-powered blender, and combine it with the raspberries and lemon juice.

Blend to combine the raspberries into the mixture, then strain the mixture through a sieve to remove the raspberry seeds.

Evenly distribute it between four 4-ounce ramekins, and chill four hours or overnight.

Store covered in the fridge up to five days.

BLUEBERRY PANNA COTTA

Prep: 10 mins

Cook/Chill: 4 hrs 10 mins

Total: 4 hrs 20 mins

Yield: 4 x 4 oz custards

Nutrition for 1 custard:

Carbs	*Fat*	*Protein*
10g	*22g*	*3g*

INGREDIENTS:

2½ tsp gelatin

2 cups full-fat coconut milk

½ tsp monk fruit powder

1 tsp vanilla

1½ cups fresh blueberries

METHOD:

Combine gelatin and coconut milk in a small saucepan, and whisk to combine. Set aside to let the gelatin soak for 5 minutes.

When the gelatin has soaked, add the monk fruit and vanilla, and whisk to combine completely.

Warm the mixture over medium heat to melt gelatin.

When the mixture is warmed, transfer it to a high-powered blender, and combine it with the blueberries.

Blend to combine the blueberries into the mixture.

Evenly distribute it between four 4-ounce ramekins, and chill four hours or overnight.

Store covered in the fridge up to five days.

VANILLA CRÈME BRÛLÉE

Prep: 10 mins

Cook: 30 mins

Total: 40 mins

Yield: 4 x 4 oz custards

Nutrition for 1 custard:

Carbs	*Fat*	*Protein*
3g	*27g*	*5g*

INGREDIENTS:

2 cups full-fat coconut milk

4 egg yolks

1 Tbsp arrowroot starch

½ tsp monk fruit powder

2 Tbsp erythritol + 1 tsp for sprinkling

1 tsp vanilla

METHOD:

Preheat the oven to 325°F. Set aside a large baking dish that can fit the four 4-ounce ramekins.

In a medium saucepan, heat the coconut milk until just steaming.

While the milk warms, combine the egg yolks, arrowroot starch, monk fruit, 2 tablespoons erythritol, and vanilla, and whisk to completely combine.

When the milk is warm, slowly add it to the yolk mixture in a steady stream, stirring constantly to temper the egg yolks.

Evenly distribute the milk mixture between four 4-ounce ramekins. Set the ramekins in the baking dish, and pour hot water into the dish around them, so the water goes halfway up the sides of the ramekins.

Bake the crème brûlée until it is set but still slightly jiggly, 30-40 minutes.

Remove the crème brûlée from the oven, and take it out of the baking dish to cool before setting it in the fridge to chill and set completely.

To Serve:

Sprinkle 1 teaspoon of erythritol over each crème brûlée.

Use a kitchen torch to caramelize the erythritol until it is golden (this may take slightly longer than with regular sugar).

Serve immediately, and enjoy!

CHOCOLATE CRÈME BRÛLÉE

Prep: 10 mins

Cook: 30 mins

Total: 40 mins

Yield: 4 x 4 oz custards

Nutrition for 1 custard:

Carbs	Fat	Protein
6g	27g	7g

INGREDIENTS:

2 cups full-fat coconut milk

4 egg yolks

6 Tbsp cacao powder

1 Tbsp arrowroot starch

½ tsp monk fruit powder

2 Tbsp erythritol + 1 tsp for sprinkling

1 tsp vanilla

METHOD:

Preheat the oven to 325°F. Set aside a large baking dish that can fit all four 4-ounce ramekins.

In a medium saucepan, heat the coconut milk until just steaming.

While the milk warms, combine the egg yolks, cacao powder, arrowroot starch, monk fruit, 2 tablespoons erythritol, and vanilla, and whisk to completely combine.

When the milk is warm, slowly add it to the yolk mixture in a steady stream, stirring constantly to temper the egg yolks.

Evenly distribute the milk mixture between four 4-ounce ramekins. Set the ramekins in the baking dish, and pour hot water into the dish around them, so the water goes halfway up the sides of the ramekins.

Bake the crème brûlée until it is set but still slightly jiggly, 30-40 minutes.

Remove the crème brûlée from the oven, and take it out of the baking dish to cool before setting it in the fridge to chill and set completely.

To Serve:

Sprinkle 1 teaspoon of erythritol over each crème brûlée.

Use a kitchen torch to caramelize the erythritol until it is golden (this may take slightly longer than with regular sugar).

Serve immediately, and enjoy!

COFFEE CRÈME BRÛLÉE

Prep: 45 mins

Cook: 30 mins

Total: 1 hr 15 mins

Yield: 4 x 4 oz custards

Nutrition for 1 custard:

Carbs	Fat	Protein
3g	27g	5g

INGREDIENTS:

2 cups full-fat coconut milk

1 Tbsp finely chopped coffee or espresso

4 egg yolks

1 Tbsp arrowroot starch

½ tsp monk fruit powder

2 Tbsp erythritol + 1 tsp for sprinkling

1 tsp vanilla

METHOD:

Preheat the oven to 325°F. Set aside a large baking dish that can fit all four 4-ounce ramekins.

In a medium saucepan, heat the coconut milk until just steaming. Add the chopped coffee or espresso beans, and set the milk aside to steep, about 30 minutes.

When the milk is done steeping, strain the chopped coffee beans, and reheat it until it is warm and just steaming again.

While the milk warms, combine the egg yolks, arrowroot starch, monk fruit, 2 tablespoons erythritol, and vanilla. Whisk to completely combine.

When the milk is warm, slowly add it to the yolk mixture in a steady stream, stirring constantly to temper the egg yolks.

Evenly distribute the milk mixture between four 4-ounce ramekins. Set the ramekins in the baking dish, and pour hot water into the dish around them, so the water goes halfway up the sides of the ramekins.

Bake the crème brûlée until it is set but still slightly jiggly, 30-40 minutes.

Remove the crème brûlée from the oven and take it out of the baking dish to cool before setting it in the fridge to chill and set completely.

To Serve:

Sprinkle 1 teaspoon of erythritol over each crème brûlée.

Use a kitchen torch to caramelize the erythritol until it is golden (this may take slightly longer than with regular sugar).

Serve immediately!

DISCOVER MORE PALEOHACKS COOKBOOKS

THE PALEO BREAKFAST BIBLE

Enjoy a variety of delicious, QUICK Paleo Breakfast Recipes (10 minutes or less!).

Give yourself an energy jump-start in the morning with Paleo alternatives to bagels, muffins, and pancakes. DON'T be stuck eating eggs and bacon every day—try our apple bread, zesty lemon scones, BBQ chicken egg muffins, and more...

With over 100 delicious breakfast recipes, you'll never run out of tasty morning meals!

Get your copy here:

http://paleobreakfastrecipes.com/

PALEO EATS

Enjoy a variety of delicious, simple, and gourmet Paleo recipes (created by Chef Peter Servold). Eat meals like Bacon Bars, Mongolian Red Pepper Beef, Pulled Pork, and over 75 more ridiculously tasty recipes.

Get the book shipped to your door for FREE—just pay shipping!

With over 80 delicious, chef-created Paleo recipes, you'll never run out of tasty meals!

Get your copy here:

http://paleorecipeteam.com/paleo-eats/

PALEO SWEETS COOKBOOK

Included are 70 delicious, nutritious Paleo-based desserts—you'd swear came from your local bakery!

Each of these recipes are all tried, tested, and family approved. Enjoy marveling at all the yummy treats, including: mouth-watering brownies, decadent cakes, delicious ice creams, crispy and chewy cookies, perfect pies, and creamy cheesecakes. With the 70 delicious recipes in *Paleo Sweets*, you and your loved ones can FINALLY enjoy your favorite desserts without the downside of traditional desserts. Get your FREE copy here (just pay shipping)!

Get your copy here:

https://www.paleorecipeteam.com/sweets/

PALEO SNACKS COOKBOOK

Eat a healthy version of all your favorite snacks with a crowd favorite: the *Paleo Snacks Cookbook*. Filled with 155 sweet and savory recipes full of gummies, apple fritters, chocolate bacon skewers, and even carrot cake, this amazing cookbook lets you satisfy your cravings guilt-free and stay healthy. Each recipe is made with 100% Paleo-friendly ingredients, which means they have no gluten, no soy, no dairy, no refined sugar, and no toxic ingredients. It's a perfect compliment to any Paleo diet, and it'll help you burn fat, boost energy, and enjoy healthy digestion.

Get your copy here:

http://www.paleorecipeteam.com/snacks

"Keep in mind that these keto-friendly recipes are still sweets, and are best eaten in moderation to help you stop craving sugar. Let these desserts simply play a part of your health journey as you cut down on those unhealthy, problematic foods. Go easy on yourself as you make the transition into keto. You're doing great!"

Kelsey Ale